Standing Up When

LIFE
FALLS DOWN
Around You

Other Books by Elizabeth B. Brown

Living Successfully with Screwed-Up People
Working Successfully with Screwed-Up People
Surviving the Loss of a Child

Standing Up When

LIFE

FALLS DOWN
Around You

Elizabeth B. Brown

Revell
a division of Baker Publishing Group
Grand Rapids, Michigan

© 2016 by Elizabeth B. Brown

Published by Revell
a division of Baker Publishing Group
P.O. Box 6287, Grand Rapids, MI 49516-6287
www.revellbooks.com

Printed in the United States of America

Library of Congress Cataloging-in-Publication Data
Names: Brown, Elizabeth B., author.
Title: Standing up when life falls down around you / Elizabeth B. Brown.
Description: Grand Rapids : Revell, 2016. | Includes bibliographical references.
Identifiers: LCCN 2016012655 | ISBN 9780800724320 (pbk.)
Subjects: LCSH: Christianity—Psychology. | Consolation.
Classification: LCC BR110 .B745 2016 | DDC 248.8/6—dc23
LC record available at https://lccn.loc.gov/2016012655

Some names and details have been changed to protect the privacy of the individuals involved.

16 17 18 19 20 21 22   7 6 5 4 3 2 1

To my BELOVED

Our cherished children
Kim, Paul III, LeeAnne, and Brad

And our grandchildren
Lauren, Ashley, Paul IV, Michael, Kaylee, and Mara Kathryn

When I sit on the porch talking to God about my life, I am going to thank Him for you.

Contents

Contents

Acknowledgments

So many deserve my gratitude for being our family's guide and support along our journey through heartache to joy. How could we have survived whole, as a family unit, and filled with joy if it had not been for you? The journey would have been so much more daunting without your sensitive, open, generous, and profound care. You held our hands, hugged, listened, and were wise with your counsel.

A special thank-you for those who read through this manuscript and offered wise advice—my husband Paul, my son Brad, my siblings Richard Bowie and Amy Williams, my granddaughter Lauren DeGennaro, and my friends Jeff Anderson, Cindy DeVane, and Karen Randall. My son Paul III saved me many times as I struggled in war with my computer. (It had a mind of its own!)

There were many who shared their stories, including Sandy Cox, Tina Thomas, Boyce Berry, John Holbrook, Michael DeGennaro, June Barrett, and Suzy Williams. The Brown Fellowship of 120 gifted me with their wisdom and tweaked critical points through discussions and study. There were also a host who simply offered encouragement and unknowingly imparted wisdom. Thank you for your part in this book.

There is no way for our family to express enough gratitude to those who have been our guides and support as we traveled through travail. Our family—close, extended, and friends broadly spread—each of you has made a significant difference in our lives. The best and most wonderful things of life cannot be seen or even touched. They are felt by the heart. Thank you!

Prologue

I write this book with aching sadness yet also with sure knowledge that doing so is a blessing. I want to share how we found our way to joy after a loss that knocked us to the ground, because someone, somewhere, doesn't feel he or she can. I am happy to tell you of the gift of faith and the blessing of caring family and friends. But, more than anything, I want to arm you with the tools that make recovery and recalibration possible. There are choices to be made in difficult times that will fill you with gratitude for life or allow you to sink further into despair.

Life has its incredible days; it also has days when it is hard to stop the flow of tears. Just keep pressing forward. A deep peace and an abiding joy can fill your spirit even in such times. Hold tight to the idiom that every day may not be good but there is something good in every day. See yourself as on a venture to find ways to overcome the hurt, not forget the past. There are ways to live with whatever has happened without hopelessness.

You may feel the world is over, just like a caterpillar locked in its cocoon. Cocoons are dark and frightening. Breaking free takes time and effort. The good news is that as a caterpillar breaks free it becomes a butterfly. It transforms from crawling in the muck to flying in the sky. So can you! I know such metamorphosis is possible.

We are programmed to work best by following the instructions of the designer. The body rights itself, the emotions balance, and with each problem overcome we become stronger and more able. Be aware that you are in a war. Battles to prevail over emotions that beg you to wallow, wail, long, and rage are hard fought. Giving up is easier—but it is not better.

This book is not filled with religious clichés or pious laws. It is about trusting God as you wonder *why*. It is about making critical choices to live victoriously instead of merely surviving. Joy comes as you choose gratitude when instead you want to despair; you must find good in the present to break the chains that bind you to the past.

Wisdom embeds. Your walk and faith become simple. You trust God's care even as you understand your choices, not a magic eraser, will wash away the anguish. Come with me as we discuss the anchors and lifelines that steady your rocking boat in life's storms.

Hang in there, friend. You are on a journey that has the power to make your life rich and deepen your appreciation for the moment. Everyone wants happiness; nobody wants pain. But you can't find the rainbows without the rain. I pray you may find hope and appreciation for your journey in *Standing Up When Life Falls Down Around You*.

Joy is a choice. It can be *your* choice. The more you sing in the rain, the less disheartening the storm.

Come. Let us share together. Time is too precious to be squandered on anguish.

1

Standing Up

What happens to you is not as important as your response to it.

■ **ANCHOR: I learn what to expect and grab the lifelines that are anchors in the storm.**

Hello, friend. I am sitting here this morning with you on my mind, wishing I could wave a wand and help you put your life back together. I'm trying to do the same with mine. Sadly, you know as well as I do that nothing can magically erase loss, injustice, unfairness, hurt, and guilt. Life must be processed, in and out, for the heart to fill with hope. This process requires intentional effort to let go of the past to find joy in the present. This is a tall order when it seems easier to give up than to stand up.

I don't know your specifics. That isn't necessary. But I do know you picked up this book because you or someone you care about is in pain; life has fallen down around you. The fallout feels heavier than you can lift and bigger than you are; your emotions are chaotic and out of control. You are knocked to the ground and recovery seems impossible. You simply aren't sure you can get back up. *Where is the hope?*

This book may help! At the very least it may arm you for future challenges, but I suspect you may be trying to navigate through a crisis now. Like me, you are probably not coping with a pull-yourself-up-by-your-bootstraps problem. This is an it's-all-over, it's-not-going-to-change, it's-ended issue or, perhaps worse, you have to live with the ongoing problem. Recovery seems daunting. Do you have the strength?

Who could understand what you feel? Who could describe the shock when you were hit out of the blue, believing all was well and then—wham! Perhaps you saw the inevitable demolition about to happen. Who would appreciate your dauntless efforts to prevent the calamity? What if, most devastating of all, you recognized the crisis gathering and prayed fervently that the collapse or injustice would not happen? Yet it did!

What do you do when what has happened cannot be reversed; when health is irreparable; when a mistake, decision, or action cannot be revoked? I've been there. Like you, I wondered *why* and wished I could turn back the clock. But now I am facing another catastrophe and this time I am armed. I first learned to travel through the rodeo of grief and its gruesome emotions by grabbing lifelines to pull myself from the devastating cocoon of longing for my daughter LeeAnne. She died from a viral encephalitis one week before her seventh birthday.

Anguish after Lee's death consumed my joy for six years. That was twenty years ago. I trusted that her death was within a greater life design, but I longed for her presence. It's not that I didn't face reality. It was not that I didn't trust God's care for our child. It was simply that time did not erase the pain of longing. During that period I spoke in conferences with thousands of families in grief, physicians, and caregivers who sought ways to recover from their personal tsunami or help others do so. I returned from each session in deeper despair as I shouldered their burden as well.

We all journey through many challenges in life. Most we handle with grace or resign ourselves to the reality after much mumbling and whining. But the truly devastating crises of life can encapsulate us for a lifetime unless we choose to let go of what is no more. Through helping so many with their struggles, I saw played out in real lives the anchors that help some stand, while others merely wrapped themselves in victimhood, even those with deep faith.

It was in writing *The Joy Choice* that I realized the length of time I rummaged in grief was a choice—my choice. I determined to choose joy. I chose to see what I had, not what was gone. I grabbed the lifelines shared in Scripture and played out in the lives of those who remained unbroken in spite of personal disaster. That doesn't mean I quit missing my daughter, especially when memories would cavort. Instead, I learned to turn missing LeeAnne into times I relished the memories. I know you are seeking the same.

Truly, knowing what to expect and how to survive deep hurt is a gift, for life is quiet only in moments. There are critical choices necessary in the midst of the horrid times in life. We must be wise, because while some choices make our situation better, others make regaining balance and finding hope more difficult.

Life doesn't remain quiet for long. We began another epic journey when Kim, our first child, began a valiant three-year struggle with leukemia in 2010. I refused to believe she would die. This was merely another life challenge. Kim had four children; she would certainly fight and win her battle with the disease. And she did fight—but she lost. She died on my birthday (more than sad!) and we were again thrown into a devastating tsunami. I knew I could choose to rail against the loss or be grateful for the time I had shared my precious daughter Kim's life. I assure you the anguish wanted to consume our beings, but as a family we chose to turn away the negative to dwell instead on the gift of her time in our lives.

Losses, injustice, and unfairness are part of life. We pray we never suffer a wound we can't survive. Regardless of how impossible it seems that you will survive this one, be assured you probably will, as most do physically. However, I believe you want more than merely to survive. You want to look forward to your day. You want to pursue the promised *abundant* life. That may seem a stretch when your mind is so connected to the past.

Remaining focused on your losses, injustice, or unfairness is like allowing your anguish to live rent free in your head.

Yet surviving while remaining focused on your losses, injustice, or unfairness is like allowing your anguish to live rent free in your head.

Perhaps surprisingly, men have a more difficult time than women during the first two years of recovery after a catastrophe. Their statistics of longevity and health plummet: four times more suicide, three times more accidents, six times more strokes, and ten times more heart attacks. Also, 40 percent seek refuge in drugs. Women fare better, at least at first, but their statistics plummet in the third year and follow much the same pattern as that of men.[1]

Why? Perhaps because from the start women let out their feelings, sharing their anguish with friends, family, and even the grocery checkout clerk. Men tend to stuff it, suck it up, and wrap themselves in armor. How can they talk it out when the classic question to a man is "How is your wife/mother/girlfriend?" Or, when on a more personal level, if he is asked "How are you?" his typical reply is "Fine" or "It's tough."

My husband, Paul, and I, like you, have confronted plenty of hurdles as we traveled life together. But each storm we handled fueled our confidence that we could weather the next. We dealt with the financial issues of a young married couple in graduate school, marriage challenges when there was only time for learning and little for loving, baby responsibilities, career shifts and moves, and then a child with chronic health problems. Most would agree that watching a child hurt is far more arduous than handling one's own pain. It certainly was for us.

We agonized for our two-year-old LeeAnne when her diabetes was declared brittle, which simply meant she hosted a multitude of complications. Still, thanks to God, she blossomed. She was a charming beacon of light. We were wrapped around her like ants on sugar. But then she was gone. I understand why many marriages crumble after a child's death. Death would have been easier than survival as a united family. It was two years before tears were not a constant companion and six years before memories brought laughter.

I was fortunate. A dear friend, Suzy Williams, offered wise counsel after LeeAnne's death. She assured me there were common elements in any disappointment or loss and she asked me to remember that, regardless of what we felt or what was expressed:

- everyone was hurting.
- no one was going crazy.
- each of us would process our pain differently.
- what each of us needed for comfort would be different.

As my emotions screamed and my thoughts seemed haywire, her words resonated. *These feelings are normal.* Knowing what I might experience was critically helpful. Recognizing differences in the ways each of us coped freed me from feeling my way of coping was also the best for others in my family. My hope is that this book will be as helpful for you as her words were to me.

Hurts bring anguish that gnaws on one's spirit, relationships, and happiness. My soul grew tired from longing for LeeAnne. It became apparent that there were only two choices: *grow bitter and wither*, hanging on to the hurts and injustice, or *survive and thrive*, thanking God for the gifts of life, both the good and the bad. I surrendered. I couldn't do it on my own, leaving God's guidance in the background. I needed a pathway to joy.

Faith offers no panacea, no quick fix for life's challenges, yet Scripture is the Designer's guide for *what works* and *what doesn't work* when life's problems cause joy's demise. The Bible is filled with stories of real people. Some valiantly overcame their problems while others wore the robe of victimhood. People today are no different. We all know those who bemoan their difficulties as if they are a badge of sainthood while others glow with an inner peace despite their problems.

I clung to Jesus's words: "I have come that they may have life, and have it to the full."[2] I wanted that! I wasn't searching for pie-in-the-sky in the afterlife. I needed help in the here-and-now. Perhaps you do too. Faith offers hope, but be assured it is also in the line of fire. You question, *If God cares, does He care about me?* and *Though He is able, is He able to help me?*

No matter the cause of our distress, our pathway back to joy requires the same things: *a choice to be grateful for what was and a decision to appreciate what is.* Of course, we cannot be grateful we were abused, our marriage ended, or our child dropped out of school. It is impossible to be happy for our war with disease or injury. Time doesn't make the hurt from the chaos of such tragedy go away. The gut-wrenchingly difficult decision to focus on the gifts of what was and the positive lessons learned through the struggle assuages our pain as it strengthens our character. Character is forged in times of challenge just as a photograph is developed in darkness.

At first I bumbled through grief's course. It was only when I shifted to focus on how blessed we were to have shared LeeAnne's life for seven years that light began to shine in my darkness. I built in little trigger thoughts—lifelines—that helped me turn away the negatives. I studied what was normal and to be anticipated. I chose to see what I had, not focus on what was no more. I chose to live with joy, even with a hole in my heart. I found anchors to steady my tilting boat.

When Kim died, we plainly hurt just as much as we did during LeeAnne's struggle for health and subsequent death, but I am handling "me" with much more wisdom. We as a family are committed to clutching the threads of recovery. I know if you are reading this book you are also seeking a path away from your anguish to a sense of joy. Recovery requires both *time* and *choice* to grasp the lifelines that anchor us in a harbor of calm.

Friend, there is good news: *you are searching for help.* You want to learn the steps to break the strangleholds that bind you in unquenchable longing or anger. That says a lot about your courage and tenacity. It takes a lot of strength to determine to work through the thoughts that want you to give up and hang on to the unchangeable. You are seeking a guide to move forward, even as you fear that very act will dishonor someone so precious to your life, let a culprit off the hook, or force you to recognize the situation is irreversible. You want to understand your programming, what to expect, and how to cope with what cannot be changed. You want justice, not revenge. You seek to find purpose, the something good that comes from overcoming bad.

> Recovery requires both time and choice to ease the hurts of life.

In *Standing Up When Life Falls Down Around You*, I'll deal with the internal storms caused by loss, injustice, and wrongs, as well as the innate power each of us has to find happiness in our midst. We will address the issues for which all of us seek insight.

- How is it possible to be happy again?
- How can I move forward when the hurt is so great?
- How do I alleviate anger or guilt that is so powerful?

- How do I calm chaotic emotions when there might not be a happily-ever-after solution?
- How do I trust God when I am struggling with doubt?

Many people do not make it out of the zone, a football term that implies a tunnel of chaos, characterized by pain. Former certainties struggle with confusion. Fear of what comes next reigns. Such times are a zone of pain. But just as in the game of football, you can break free and make it to your goal line.

There is no question—happiness is an easier choice for someone splashing in puddles than for someone drowning in a swamp. Fortunately, there is wisdom that can guide you through the choices necessary to pull you from any waters, no matter their depth. I have intentionally addressed some of these concepts several times. Some are too critical to recovery to overlook. Hopefully, repeating these lifelines will highlight their importance.

If you are muddling with an issue addressed in a chapter, read the chapter several times. Highlight a phrase that addresses your need. Write out a plan to address the issue. Underline an anchor. Hold tight to the lifelines to recovery. Handling a crisis in life requires courage, determination, and intention. I hope you are coping rather than muddling as you deal with your tsunami.

Happiness is an easier choice for someone splashing in puddles than for someone drowning in a swamp.

Be warned: all tough times put you at a crossroad where you choose either to be responsible for thoughts and decisions that incite your emotions or to join the ranks of those who drape themselves in black. One path leads you toward an abiding sense of joy, even with the challenge of great hurts. The other path holds tight to the past and its anguish, guaranteeing a lifetime of pain not only for yourself but also for those who care about the wounded. You may have taken some vicious hits. A good share of us have serious pain—health issues, divorce, addiction, wretched children, a despondent spouse, or low self-esteem. Guilt. Loneliness. You may have started with good intentions but became blindsided along the way. Still, it is true that all in life lasts for but a season. As you know the sun will rise, so also believe that this period of hurt will end. It was always so. It will always be. Recognize that just as seasons change, you, too, are in a process of change.

Recovering after a stunning blow begins with your own desire for a life that is not just lived on the surface but is rich and deep and high and wide. Come, let's journey together so that you will change for the better, not the bitter.

LIFELINES

1. Life doesn't stay quiet long.
2. Abundant life is for now, not just the afterlife.
3. Faith offers no panacea, no quick fix, just a guidebook of choices for *what works* and *what doesn't*.
4. It is choice, not just time, that eases the hurts of life.
5. Happiness is an easier choice for someone splashing in puddles than for someone drowning in a swamp.

2

Facing Your Giant

If you do not believe you can win, you will lose
your battle!

■ **ANCHOR: I have been in training to win all my life!**

*How can I do this? I am unable. I am too small, too weak, and
too hurt. This is bigger than me.*

Fighting "giants" is a story plot that has always inspired and encouraged. It is the epic drama of the little guy in battle against an
awesomely powerful villain. Each giant tale is one of good news:
against all odds, the little guy can win. That message touches
a chord in all of us because battling our giants is an unwanted
but unavoidable part of life. We find ourselves in battle with
losses, injustices, health issues, addictions, and other wrongs,
biggies that cause us to question our strength to win against such
a force.

The historic war saga of the shepherd boy David pitted against the giant Goliath is a tale of a battle between the tribe of Israel and the mighty Philistines. The Philistines were a seafaring people from the Greek isles who sailed across the Mediterranean Sea to settle along the coast of what today is Israel. They wanted to establish a trade route across the Middle East and into the Orient.

The Philistines were sophisticated warriors in a time when those with the best weapons won, one killing at a time. They had not only the best equipment and battle-tested soldiers but also Goliath, a man whose size and strength were daunting. They wanted the land held by the Israelites for their trade route. The Israelites were afraid.

The battle lines were drawn in the Valley of Elah, a plain between the shore held by the Philistines and the mountain home of the Israeli tribes. This flat area is where conflicts were settled for centuries. It was where the knights of the Crusades fought a long, losing battle in the twelfth century against Saladin, leader of the Muslims, to reclaim Jerusalem for the Christians. Even today it is an area where Israel has missile sites that keep terrorists at bay.

The ancient wars were not the push-button type of today. Battles were won either in a blood bath or by agreement to a duel to the death between a fighter from each side of the conflict. The Philistine general chose the mighty warrior Goliath to broadcast the challenge—"Choose a man and have him come down to me. If he is able to fight and kill me, we will become your subjects; but if I overcome him and kill him, you will become our subjects and serve us."[1]

The Israelites were a short people, averaging no more than five and a half feet tall, except for their king, a man who stood a head taller than his subjects. Who volunteers to battle when the odds are so stacked against him? Not even a king! This is where the story gets good. The little guy steps out. David, a teenager who herded sheep for his family, volunteered. "Send me," he said. "I'll fight and win."

David was unimportant, too young to join the military and fight for his country. The gasps were audible. The distraught soldiers knew David had no chance. They felt doomed. Surely his bravado was out of sync with reality. Their pleas wrapped him in warnings and advice: you aren't trained for such combat; you aren't worthy; don't get involved; run and hide.

Are family and friends afraid for you as David's were for him, and as mine were for our family when we faced our giant? Are their voices of woe pleading "How can you survive?" Do they plead for you to give up on your marriage, move in with your parents, sell your home, or quit your job? Are they pushing you to fight for justice or to just get even?

I wonder if David questioned whether he could win. Was he concerned that those whose profession was war, the old guys, might know best when the king recommended he wear heavy armor? Did the soldiers' fear cause David to doubt his ability? Was he worried that his slingshot was too unsophisticated? Or was he confident that with God's help he would win against this enemy as he had against a bear and a lion while shepherding sheep?

Who feels ready to fight their battles? I was overwhelmed when my two-year-old child was diagnosed with diabetes. A kind nurse demonstrated how to prick LeeAnne's finger to draw blood and check it in a glucometer. She talked about insulin and food, and rattled on about what to do if Lee couldn't be aroused from sleep.

I considered running away with my two-year-old. But when her problems exacerbated to include epilepsy and rheumatic pains, I knew though I might complain, stomp, and try to deny the problem, I had to put on my big girl pants and don a nurse's cap to partner in her critical care. Though I was not a bit medical, I can assure you that with each successive medical crisis I became more experienced at knowing when to react, who to call for help, and how to discern the critical from the noncritical.

LeeAnne's death from a simple virus stunned me. I was back to square one, wishing I could run away and deny the reality. I had no inkling of how to handle my longing. How could I win against the anguish? Of course, I would survive, but would I ever feel happiness and joy? Seriously? The good news is I do—and you can, too, if you do it the way David did!

David clearly stated his advantages:

- I have already defeated fierce foes, a lion and a bear.
- I trust my ability.
- I am not in the battle alone.

Could it be that you, just like David, have been in training through skirmishes, hurts, and losses in life to overcome the hurdles and roadblocks of your catastrophe? Have you learned what to do or what not to do from others who fought their giants? Have you observed and stored tips to help you in your battle as you read Scripture? Have you listened to personalities like Dr. Phil for tips on handling problems, or watched movies such as *Unbroken*, the inspiring and heroic story of Louie Zamperini's survival against all odds in the Japanese prison camps? Overcoming is an unpleasant but critical part of recalibrating after crisis.

When Facing Your Giant, Your Tactics Must Fit Your Strengths

Goliath wanted the battle to be up close and personal. He wanted hand-to-hand combat, for he believed no one could win against his power. He was covered with a hundred pounds of armor and carried a sword, spear, and javelin, more than enough weaponry to do the job. But historians suggest that Goliath, like many who grow out of proportional height, had a health problem—acromegaly due to pituitary tumors that cause overgrowth and weakened vision stemming from compressed optic nerves.[2] Perhaps that is why a shield barrier led Goliath to the battle site, where he called for David to come to him.

As both armies surrounded the designated battleground, Goliath watched David's approach with contempt. The youth walked toward him with his walking stick instead of a sword. "Am I a dog?" he roared at David, "that you come at me with sticks?"[3] Where were David's weapons? I imagine that is when Goliath saw the sling. Scorn morphed into fear.

Though it seemed the youth was the underdog, Goliath recognized David had a clear advantage. David had a sling. A rock slung from a slingshot can cover thirty-four meters per second, hitting a target two football fields away with the same impact as a .45 magnum.[4] Goliath knew his size was no advantage against David's shot to an uncovered spot on his head. His only hope was that David would miss his target.

Malcolm Gladwell, in his book *David and Goliath*, said there is an important lesson as we battle giants: *the powerful and the strong are not always what they seem*. It is important to note that we also *may not be what we feel*—weak and ill-prepared to meet our challenge. Like David, we have been in training for such a time as this. You may feel unable but you are not. Life has afforded you many opportunities to work through difficulties.

Think about people you know who have been valiant in their battles. Journal whether their strengths were specifically targeted for resolution of their crisis—or did the issue bow, as did Goliath, to something unexpected? Write remembrances of times you gained insight and training to enable you to stand against a foe. You may be prepared in ways you had not considered. Be assured, you are here for a mission that needs your particular skills, just as the battle with Goliath needed someone who could sling a rock.

A woman approached me after a seminar. She stated to get it together and move on after your spouse dies, your no. burns down, or your job is cut, but my problem is different because there is no end to my mother's complaints. If she would just change, then I could be happy." I thought *This is her giant*. I asked, "What if your mother never changes? Are you going to be unhappy for the rest of your life?"

This woman spinning around her mother was my impetus for writing *Living Successfully with Screwed-Up People*. Counting on someone else to change so you can be happy is like fighting Goliath on his terms. You'll never win. You can't base how you feel on whether others do

> *The powerful and the strong are not always what they seem; neither are we what we feel—weak and ill-prepared.*

what you think best or your life experiences are happy. Happiness is a choice to see the good in life regardless of the problems.

That young woman needed the same things as you and I do. She needed to recognize that she was responsible to strategize and set boundaries in her relationships. She was allowing herself to twist around another individual's acts. She wanted change. The good news is that if she refused to spin around her parent, the relationship would change regardless of her mother's behavior. Determining to control yourself is the key to moving forward in life's challenges.

Does refusing to spin around our difficulties or irregular relationships mean life will be rosy, with no problems or pain? Of course not. But it does mean we have power, regardless of our woe, to find gifts in our situation. The young woman with the difficult mother might discern that it is not the problems in life that determine her joy; it is her reaction to the problems. What a valuable lesson! Are you seeking to discern lessons as you meet your challenge?

It takes courage to face your giant, especially when it is a Goliath-sized, life-shattering crisis that makes us feel unable. I am a teacher. My skills are certainly not medical, but the skill I needed most when confronting LeeAnne's health problems was not knowledge of the medical facts but rather the confidence to believe that I could help my child deal with the ups and downs of her problems. Medical procedures can be learned. I imagine you are trying to ferret out your strengths. You may need to do something that seems as far from your skillset as mine seemed to be from being a home-care nurse. Think through your skills. Each of us has intangible traits not listed in our academic or job résumé. Our past experiences are a training ground.

Happiness is a choice to see the good in life regardless of the problems.

A widow shared that her husband had been the social butterfly in their family. She felt lost after his death and backed away from social activities for quite a while, until finally she faced the fact that she would be a lonely old couch potato, watching television and licking her wounds, if she didn't get out of the house. She described her first social interactions at church and clubs as painful, but the more she went, the more she became interested in others and less self-focused. "Now," she said, with a laugh, "friends tell me I am far more outgoing than my husband was." You may be surprised, as was this widow, that you are far more able than you believe yourself to be.

Slow Down

When facing life's challenges, we must pause to balance *hopelessness* with *hope*. This requires that we see our options clearly, not with rose-colored optimism that denies reality. David was not foolish. He trusted he was able to win because of his life training. He also recognized he was not in the battle alone. He didn't listen to the voices begging him to give up. Because he was willing to meet his challenge, his virtues grew: confidence, resilience, discipline, patience, and courage.

Come on, friend! Be encouraged; the human spirit is incredibly resilient. Let's refuse to bow to life's problems. Stand tall. It will be exciting to look back, like that widow, and recognize we have become stronger and more able because we trusted our life training that enabled us to fight our giants. Let's join hands and cheer each other onward, knowing difficulties offer the possibility of a new, better self as we bravely face our upheavals. *God changes caterpillars into butterflies, sand into pearls, and coal into diamonds with time and pressure.*[5] With His care we can be strong.

LIFELINES

1. Life doesn't stay quiet long.
2. Abundant life is for now, not just the afterlife.
3. Faith offers no panacea, no quick fix, just a guidebook of choices for *what works* and *what does not.*
4. Recovery requires both time and choice to ease the hurts of life. Happiness is an easier choice for someone splashing in puddles than for someone drowning in a swamp.

3

Finding Your Way

Taking Responsibility for Your Recovery

It's not the size of the dog in the fight that is as important as the size of the fight in the dog.

Dwight Eisenhower

■ ANCHOR: I refuse to be destroyed by my catastrophe!

Let go. You have to let go. The pain won't stop until you release wanting what is no more, what is gone! The words echoed between my silent screams. Never! How can I turn loose? If I let go, it will be over. My life will be over. . . .

There is life after tragedy. But when distress eats every thought and steals hope, when you wonder how you can go on or what you should do to right the wrong, you are faced with your first decision on the journey back to inner contentment: to succumb to your screaming emotions or to fight through the anguish to recover your sense of joy and peace. There is no middle ground. It is an either-or situation.

The first year is a struggle. You are fatigued from acting "normal" during the day as your mind cavorts with memories. At night you lie in bed, awaiting blessed sleep, drained, wanting "out" for a few hours. Nothing doing. The quiet allows the memories to play like a scratched record, running pell-mell into chaos.

The American Psychiatric Association states that being absorbed in your hurt should end in about three months, but previous generations have known to allow themselves leeway to mourn and wear black for a year. During the first year it is *normal* to wrap one's self in longing for what was, to be filled with thoughts of revenge for injustice and justifying wrongs, and to wallow in unadulterated anguish. The holidays and special days arrive laden with memories that must be survived. You begin to regain your footing as the months pass, but as D-day's anniversary draws near you are again on a slippery slope. You become weepy, sad, and testy.

The critical first decision you must make when trying to recover from a hurt is to refuse the terrible life event the power to consume you.

Sam remembered the first anniversary after his divorce. He chose to accept a speaking engagement, thinking it would be good to have a focus. As the day approached, he was overcome with anxiety. Thinking was difficult, ideas flighty. A weight inside pulled, making it difficult for him to feel anything except heaviness and longing.

The anniversary of his divorce that he tried to "forget" was almost as difficult as the day the judge approved the settlement that ended his thirty-five-year marriage. He was two people—Sam who was greeting people in the conference room and Sammy who was grieving. Sammy longed for his wife and their old life.

It was interesting to be two people at one time. Sam's words came out as he focused, but Sammy was numb. Sam was functioning, Sammy was longing—connected by the gut-wrenching pain in his stomach.

The good news is that it is not inevitable to stay locked in the past. You can refuse that undeniably terrible hurt the power to consume you, even though at times you feel split in two. There is hope.

The second year in many ways is easier because you survived the first. That first year was filled with holidays and special memory times. You didn't go "crazy." The down times grow further apart. But do they evaporate? No! Healing takes time and requires you to refuse to allow your crisis to destroy you as you work through the consuming emotions.

The Difficult Journey

Determining our actions and attitude, even in the midst of serious problems, is a choice. Being young, middle aged, or old does not make you better at handling life's catastrophes. Our two-year-old daughter LeeAnne was miserable for a year after her diabetes onset. She wanted nothing to do with shots, food restrictions, or the myriad medical interventions. We thought two was too young to fully understand. Still, her diabetes was not going away. She had to choose her attitude, so we encouraged her. "Lee, you have a health problem. The medicines will help you feel better, but you have to decide whether you are going to be happy, even with your problem, or if you are going to let diabetes make you unhappy. Happy or grumpy—your choice." One morning after the "pep talk," her attitude was changed. She determined to be happy, regardless of her fragile health and hospitalizations.

Dogged determination is critically needed in order to refuse catastrophe the power to destroy your joy. Many make heroic decisions to find a way from tragedy to a full and rewarding life. David Pelzer, severely abused as a child, had plenty of reasons to give up on happiness. Before he was taken from his dysfunctional home to safety, he was verbally abused, was brutally beaten, was starved, and survived his mentally ill mother's attempts to kill him.

Once, when he had been stabbed in the stomach with a kitchen knife by his mother, he dragged himself to his father for help. His father lowered his voice, and said, "I tell you what; you go back in there and do the dishes. I won't even tell your mother that you told, okay? This will be our little secret. Go on now, before she catches the both of us."[1]

David did what most of us do as we try to figure out how to survive our difficulties. He tried to be better, begged, and hid. He recalled the night he determined to win the struggle with his mother, not just dogpaddle in the chaos. His mother locked him in the bathroom, leaving a deadly cocktail of ammonia and Clorox. Choking and feeling death's hand, David heard a voice. *David, cover your mouth and nose with a wet cloth*. He survived because he obeyed that quiet voice inside and covered his face. Lying on the floor, he determined: *I will not let her kill me*. He was six years old. Is your spirit whispering to you?

Emotional scars do *not* heal on their own or with time. Even after he was awarded the title of Most Outstanding Young Person of the World, David had a self-esteem buried under years of being told he was worthless. In a conference with others who had suffered childhood abuse, he described his journey to forgive his parents, overcome entrenched guilt for his failure to be loved, and stop the games he played to try to earn love. He described the mammoth effort to heal. He declared that his terrible childhood, just as theirs, gave him rare insights, strength, and a determination to live life fully. "I'm so blessed. The challenges of my past have made me immensely strong inside. . . . From the time in the bathroom when I almost died and throughout the challenges I faced, the good Lord was always over my shoulder, giving me quiet encouragement and strength when I needed it most. I am happy and free because I trust that I survived because God has a purpose for my life—just as he has for yours."[2]

The appreciation of one's life purpose often arises from the ashes of a life crisis. Recorded in the Bible thousands of years ago is the story of Joseph, the young and privileged son of the wealthy nomadic tribal leader Jacob. Joseph's brothers, overcome by jealousy, plot to kill him. Instead they sell him into slavery to a passing Egyptian caravan.

Healing requires a refusal to allow anyone or any hurt to deaden your spirit.

Joseph battles his hurt to meet his servitude to the best of his abilities. As the wealthy captain of Pharaoh's guards, Potiphar recognizes Joseph's diligence and competence and rewards him, appointing him head of his estate. Can you imagine how Joseph praised God for this opportunity? Then Joseph, perhaps like you and me, finds himself again facing another woe. Potiphar's wife falsely accuses him of attacking her. His fortune reversed, he describes his unjust situation as being "in a pit."

It is difficult to pick yourself up by the bootstraps and move on. It is a choice that must be made by each of us repeatedly as we meet the challenges of life. Joseph persevered, overcoming a multitude of obstacles in his path, until at the age of thirty he wielded power over all of Egypt, seated beside Pharaoh. He oversaw the warehousing of Egypt's grain for seven years in preparation for famine.

James Bond movies hold no more intrigue than Joseph's story. Wealthy, powerful Joseph is overcome by emotion when his brothers come to purchase food for their starving nomadic tribe. Imagine his conflicted emotions! He held these scoundrels' lives in his hand. Did he want revenge? Did he want to see his brothers experience the anguish he had? The plot thickens as Joseph implicates his brothers in thievery and spying.

Perhaps you hold the power to destroy someone who hurt you. Your decision, just as Joseph's, of how to handle the situation will affect not only you but also generations to come. Joseph's story ends with his choice to refuse to carry his anger anymore. Behind closed doors he weeps so loudly his servants are fearful, spreading concern throughout his household. It isn't easy for any of us to let go of the hurts of our catastrophe. It is painful. We can cry, stomp, and wail, but we must let it go if we want to be free of its burden.

> *The appreciation of one's life purpose often arises from the ashes of life crisis.*

Joseph wiped his face, swollen by tears, before he told his astonished brothers who he was. He called to them.

> Come close to me. . . . I am your brother Joseph, the one you sold into Egypt! And now, do not be distressed and do not be angry with yourselves for selling me here, because it was to save lives that God sent me ahead of you. . . . God sent me ahead of you to preserve for you a remnant on earth and to save your lives by a great deliverance. So then, it was not you who sent me here, but God.[3]

Setting Your Goal

Overcoming the emotions that want to bind you is a battle that can be won. The first step is refusing to surrender to the issue that threatens to destroy you. *I will not let this destroy my family. . . . I refuse to let the behavior of this person make me bitter. . . . I will not believe I am of no value because of the comments of another. . . . I will not be unhappy forever because someone I love is gone.*

Refusing to be destroyed by tragedy has two parts: first, deciding to fight the emotions that beg you to give up; second, setting goals for the long-term best. Setting your goal for the long term is not easy when emotions beg for a "feel good" now. Most of life's problems are not a black-and-white issue. Finding balance between an aging parent's need to be independent and his or her safety and protection is difficult. Staying the course in a difficult relationship may be best for the sake of others. Moving to where children live when one's partner dies is debatable. Loaning our adult children money is questionable. Fighting for grandparent rights may hurt the grandchildren more than help.

The manner in which we handle dilemmas such as these affects our present and future. Being realistic, praying for guidance, and developing a plan free you from knee-jerk reactions. You no longer waffle or give in to your emotions or the pleas of others.

Once you experience being freed from begging, berating, or longing, just as David Pelzer and Joseph, you will never allow anything—or anyone—to hold your spirit captive. Consider these first steps toward freedom:

- Refuse to allow this crisis the power to destroy your joy.
- Look at the situation realistically.
- Pray for wisdom.
- Set your goal for the long-term best.
- Develop your plan.

Let's talk more about what to expect and how to cope with emotions that beg for our attention in the midst of chaos. The more we understand our emotions and normal reactions, the more our vision clears and allows us to move toward our goals in the midst of difficult problems. The more we appreciate that *we are responsible for our actions*, the less we feel controlled by the actions of others.

Is it really possible that difficulty "makes you better" or that "God will never give you more than you can handle"? Ask anyone in the midst of their difficulties if they consider their plight to be constructive, and I imagine the answer is simply another question: Who in their right mind thinks pain is positive?

LIFELINES

1. The critical first decision you must make when trying to recover from a hurt is to refuse the undeniably terrible life event the power to consume you.

2. Significant hurts are binding but cannot imprison your joy unless you allow them that power.

3. Your spirit whispers hope and ways to recover.

4. If you don't have a plan, you flounder or make knee-jerk responses when emotions are stirred.

5. A plan will help you feel less reactive and more in control of yourself.

4

When Pain Is
a Good Thing

Warning: life without pain could really hurt you.

■ **ANCHOR: I give thanks for the pain.**

The pain is so intense. Someone is dragging a knife through me, turning it, ripping me! No! It isn't a knife. It is a scream. A scream tears my body apart, pushing, filling my head until a low wail escapes. Convulsive heaves change to dry, wrenching vomiting. I feel tired, dull, lifeless. The silence is crashing like thunder. The scream begins again.

Sleep is gone. The endless nights are filled with fragmented thoughts, questions, wet pillowcases. Paul and I cling together, holding each other. His quiet sobs alternate with mine. The emptiness is a black hole that sucks our strength, consumes our emotions. It eats more voraciously in the stillness.

Is this just a dream? No. Dreams are not like this. Nightmares are not like this. They end. Tonight I relive choosing an outfit for Lee's burial—for the thousandth time. The thoughts are like a McDonald's sign—We sold 1 million hamburgers, 2 million. . . . I pick out the treasured purple, long dress with the pink sash, little crocheted socks with flowers. She wore that special dress to school, to church, to be a fairy princess. I add her soft Care Bear with the big heart. She would want something to cuddle. The sick feeling that filled my stomach when we left the dress at the funeral home begins again. Tonight makes 1,001. God, I can't stand this! Why didn't you save our little girl? I want her.[1]

Friends, who can describe the pain when your love walks out, your child dies, you are fired, a friend is disloyal, someone you care about is an addict, or you are diagnosed with a disease? At first, there is shock. *It couldn't be true.* Then comes the bargaining and begging. *Please, I'll do anything.* Then the crushing reality. *It isn't going to change.*

We knew our second daughter to face death would not die. Though Kim's chance of surviving leukemia was slim, surely God would not allow us to face such pain again. Kim had four children of her own. She was a valiant fighter. Multiple times she pulled back from death's door. She seemed so much better at Christmas. Our entire family went to a tree farm for Christmas trees, celebrated at the Biltmore, and opened gifts. Then the slide began again. The afternoon she died I was returning from the grocery store when, a mile from Kim's home, an ambulance pulled in front of my car, its siren blasting. I knew. Cold filled my soul. *No, no!* But it was so.

Do you remember the moment your anguish from the injustice or loss consumed you? The pain filled every crevice of your being during the day. The endless nights stole your sleep. The days floated on never-ending questions. What could have prevented the crisis?

How can the injustice be righted? Who can survive this? Who could say thank you for the pain?

Dr. Paul Brand, a world-renowned physician who has studied pain, declares pain is crucial. He clearly illustrates his paradigm shift from perceiving pain as something to be rid of to an awareness of its gift. A young mother brought her precious and impish four-year-old child to him for help. The child, Tanya, bounced into his office, laughing, followed by her mother who seemed in despair. "Help her," the mother pleaded.

Tanya's feet and several fingers were wrapped in gauze. Unwrapping the blood-soiled bandages, Dr. Brand found her foot to be grossly infected with ulcers and soft, necrotic tissue, even areas of bare bone. Regardless of the probing, Tanya showed no reaction. Her foot rotated freely, the sign of a fully dislocated ankle. He winced at the unnatural movement, but Tanya did not. The tips of her fingers were gnawed off but she expressed no anguish when touching objects.

Neither parent realized Tanya had a problem until she was about eighteen months old. Tanya's mother found her sitting on the floor of the playpen, her finger painting red swirls on the white plastic sheets. "I didn't grasp the situation at first, but when I got closer I screamed," she said. "The tip of Tanya's finger was mangled and bleeding. She had bitten off her finger's tip. It was her own blood she was using to make those designs on the sheets."[2]

Her parents' horror turned to despair as wounds mysteriously appeared on one finger after another. Spankings and other physical threats had no effect on stopping the game. Feet also became a problem when Tanya learned to walk. She would step on a nail and not bother to pull it out. If she twisted her ankle she didn't limp, so she twisted it again and again. She refused to wear shoes, tore off her bandages, even ripped open a plaster cast with her bare hands. The father deserted the family, announcing, "We've begotten a monster."[3]

42

Tanya was healthy in every respect but one: she did not feel pain. Nerves in her hand transmitted messages about changes in pressure and temperature—she felt a kind of tingling when she bit her finger or burned it—but these were not unpleasant sensations. In fact she seemed to enjoy the tingling sensations, especially when they produced such dramatic reactions in others. She was not a monster, only an extreme example of life without physical pain. Being born without pain sensors literally crippled her.

The Good and Bad of Pain

No one wants pain. Yet the story of little Tanya illustrates the need for a degree of physical pain. Without the ability to sense pain, her physical body was unprotected from harm. We might ask if pain is also important for our spiritual development. *Does the emotional pain that is born as we deal with crisis act as a sifter to prioritize the important in our life from the unimportant, the good from the bad, and the helpful from the harmful?* Pain is crucial for our physical well-being, emotional maturation, and spiritual growth. Facing and surmounting difficulties helps us build confidence, strategies for maneuvering through problems, and the sense that we can overcome. As we cope with

If you do not feel pain when things are askew, you will not be healthy in body, mind, or spirit.

our tsunamis we have the opportunity to grow a deeper appreciation for the good in life, our supporting family and friends, and a faith that weathers the storms. Our choice in reaction to the pain determines whether we will find peace and joy even in the midst of problems or will be filled with anxiety, bitterness, anger, or guilt.

The problem is our thoughts and emotions wage war against our spirit in times of overwhelming anguish. God designed us to be ruled by the spirit, but it is humanity's natural tendency to feed the body and starve the spirit as our emotions beg for attention. Therefore, we become imprisoned in our wounds.

It is as if our spirit asks us to do exactly the opposite of what feels natural. Our thoughts beg to get even when hurt. Our emotions cry, *You hurt me; I'll punch you back!* or *I want it; I'll get it.* In contrast, the whispers of our spirit ask our emotions to do what is right in God's eyes, regardless of our feelings. It encourages us to hope in hopeless situations and believe that good can come from even such as this. It whispers, *You hurt me; I will forgive*, and *This is unspeakably difficult, but I will trust.*

Following our emotions imprisons and paralyzes us; following God's counsel brings hope and frees us when all seems hopeless.

Our Interconnected Systems

Most of us know a great deal about the physical side of our body. We understand the importance of eating right and exercising. We recognize pain in our body means a problem. But, we may not be aware that our being is comprised of three systems that have very different ways of handling emotional and physical pain, yet each affects the other. We are a unit of body, mind, and

Our Interconnected Systems

- **Mind**—the control center and gateway for our thoughts, emotions, and responses.
- **Body**—two separate, unique functioning components: our physical self and our emotions.
- **Spirit**—the voice within that encourages response to pain for long-term good.

The Mind

- The mind responds to physical pain automatically and reflexively.
- Physical pain has a fade factor.
- The mind's response to emotional pain requires conscious direction.
- Emotional pain has no fade factor.

spirit—just as a candle is a unit comprised of three: body, flame, and product.

Consider a candle. It has a *body* made of wax with a wick, a *flame* that produces a product, and the *product* of heat and light. There is never a time when you can have the candle with its flame without producing heat and light, nor is there a time when you have heat and light without the body of wax and wick. Each part is a separate entity that affects and is affected by the others—the more physical flame, the more heat and light; the less heat and light, the less physical flame.

In the same way as a candle is composed of separate functions that make the whole, we are also one—mind, body with physical and emotional compartmentalization, and spirit. Whatever affects one system also affects the others. The mind is the gateway that allows the cognition of pain. It responds differently to physical pain through automatic programming. Emotional pain requires conscious decisions. It is in these conscious decisions that we feel the interplay of our spirit. Let's think how each functioning system copes with pain when our world falls apart.

Our mind responds to physical pain *automatically* in ways to catalyst healing and resolve the pain. If you slice your finger while cutting fruit, the body *reflexively* recoils, pulling your hand away from the knife before a sense of pain registers in your brain. Without any conscious thought, cells gather fluid to flush out the cut, other cells flood the cut to form a scab, and healing begins. As soon as the finger heals, you forget about the hurt.

The mind automatically attempts to alleviate and eliminate physical problems with its arsenal of chemicals and hormones. Tears are an example of the body's efficiency and positive directed response to specific problems. Tears caused by cutting onions are 98 percent water. In contrast, tears caused by stress contain high levels of the toxins that have been released into the blood and lymphatic systems by stress's effect. That is why people often say they feel relieved after crying.

- Basal tears wash the eyeball with antibodies that target micro-organisms and defend against pathogens.
- Irritant tears wash away debris such as dust.
- Emotional tears that contain proteins release hormones and chemicals that are elevated to high levels under stress.

Another remarkable characteristic of the mind's reaction to physical pain is its unique *fade factor*. A classic example of this is childbirth. A mother in delivery may vow to have no more children, but with time she forgets the pain's intensity and longs for another child. The memory of pain fades with time and healing.

The mind acts as a *gateway* that triages physical and emotional pain in order of urgency. For example, a mother who hears both her infant's cry and her two-year-old child's urgent scream triages her response to interpret which is the more desperate need. You may recall stories of soldiers disregarding limbs shattered by gunfire in battle in order to drag a fallen comrade to safety. Such is possible because of the mind's ability to gateway a friend's safety as the more urgent problem to resolve.

Yet though the mind has an incredible ability to stabilize and correct physical problems, prolonged stress has innumerable negative

Emotions of the Body

- Resolutions of emotional pain require a conscious decision to act.
- The mind has no fade factor for emotional pain.

effects such as elevated blood pressure, headaches, ulcers, heart issues, and psychosomatic disorders. T-cell production lowers, affecting the immune system. Perhaps you recall feeling sluggish or ill after a period of emotional chaos. The sense is not just psychological. Your body becomes more susceptible to viruses and bacteria when its chemicals are out of balance.

Unlike the mind's automatic response to physical pain, every response and action of the mind to emotions is directed by the individual's evaluation of the situation. Simply stated, *what we think is as important to our emotions and thoughts as what we eat is to our physical body*. Likewise, thoughts and emotions directly affect the physical body and spirit. If we dwell on the negative,

guilt morphs into shame,

anger grows into rage,

love turns into hatred,

loss strengthens into longing,

injustice seeks revenge, and

the body and spirit succumb to depression, ill-health, and spiritual malaise.

Though the emotions tied to memories stored in the mind may lessen over time, a traumatic experience can be recalled with its accompanying pain-filled emotions until the mind has been directed to let it go (forgive) or the hurt is turned into gratitude for the lessons learned. This is a crucial understanding. Your life calamity can be used as a rationale for victimhood for as long as you choose to allow it to dominate your thoughts. You can't stop it playing repeatedly and violently immediately following the tragedy. Time is required to ease the stress. But it is a choice to forgive and let go as you find ways to be thankful that turn the trauma into an awareness of the preciousness of life, the gifts of friendship and family, and the treasure of the moment.

Our spirit is often defined as our essence—zest, enthusiasm, or depression. Yet we wonder if the spirit is more than a description of personality as we hear tales of something separate arising from the body after death, or sense a thought that seems distinct and counter to our logic or emotions. Sometimes we seem to just know, though we do not understand how we know. Some experience a command that is unexplainable but compels them to action. The spirit within is thought to be a mystery, a sudden sure knowledge, a whispered suggestion, or a sense of hope beyond reason. Those of faith label this nebulous sense that functions separately from the body and mind as God working within us. This unexplainable sense within us seems to urge action, encourage us, offer hope,

The Spirit

The Spirit encourages us:

to accept responsibility for our actions and responses.
to acknowledge and apologize when we do wrong so
  we are free from hiding or self-abasement.
to not feel guilty for someone else's choice.
to believe that God works all things together for good,
  even devastating circumstances.
to trust God's care.

even command actions that are distinct or counter to our logic or emotion.

Have you ever felt a sudden urge to contact someone, lock a door, or change your plans? The more we trust this sense, the more powerful its guidance seems to be.

The sense does not have to be about a critical issue. A teacher planned an outdoor play for presentation by her kindergarten in a month when rain was an everyday occurrence. She felt certain—a sure knowledge—that it would not rain the day of the play. Despite her feeling, as the rainy days continued she rented an indoor auditorium because such belief seemed illogical with the continued downpour. The day of the play it was sunny and not a drop of rain fell. She explained, "I felt it would not rain, but it seemed so illogical that I simply couldn't take the chance!" But it is powerful when we do take the chance. Our faith is awakened.

Shifting Focus

It is critically important that we do not stay stuck in anguish when we travel through travail. No question, we will grieve for what is gone, lost, or unjust. We must find ways to counter the negative thoughts that will affect our well-being. When we confront issues that are painful by dwelling on thoughts such as, *Why did this happen to me? I don't deserve this. It isn't fair!* or *I'm no good so God is punishing me*, our mind is filled with anger and regret. Our outlook becomes imprisoned in defeat, shame, and bitterness. Physical changes in chemicals, hormones, and electromagnetic charges eventually become a vast array of health issues.

It seemed an eternity before I turned my longing for my daughter LeeAnne to gratitude to God for the years she and I shared. Though I believed that her death was within God's will, I missed her and dwelt on her absence. Of course, hanging on for six years after her death was harmful. I lost my zest—my spirit. I focused on what was wrong with life—my mind and emotions; I had a stroke—my body.

I did not realize I held the power to control my focus. It seemed impossible to turn from longing for what-was-no-more to appreciation for what-had-been. Is it possible to shift our focus from the hurt of divorce to the strength in commitment? Can we turn from pitying our childhood's dysfunctional home life to recognizing those problems have bred in us a strong determination to have a loving family? Is it possible, when struggling with pain, to be grateful for the time our life was pain free?

Gratitude to God is the single most important controllable response that nourishes health and keeps you from sinking into an abyss.

Of course it is possible! There is only one option to keep a difficult situation from becoming worse: turn away the negative. Grab lifelines, trust God's care, pray, and force yourself to do right, regardless of what others do.

Let me repeat, and please, heed this warning: physical health reacts and is subject to emotions. Focusing on the negative intensifies emotional pain and unlocks a Pandora's box of ill health. Find a way to turn from longing, anger, hurt, or anguish for the sake of your well-being.

Of course, you and I know that just thinking happy thoughts or being grateful will not completely stop the pain from bouncing in and out of our mind as we battle difficulties. But it does keep us from sinking into a deep darkness.

It is not our *recognition* of pain but rather our *response* to it that determines our journey. Our response either sweetens our temper, stifles our anger, buries our envy, bridles our tongue, restrains our hand, and fills us with gratitude as it emboldens our spirit to trust God's care—or not!

I knew what to expect when my daughter Kim died. I had traveled the journey. I knew from firsthand experience that stress would open my body to another health crisis and my mind to depression. With each pang of longing, I stopped my swirling thoughts and said, "Thank you that it hurts. That means I had a special relationship and lots of love." Gratitude changed anguish to appreciation. Gratitude to God is the single most important controllable response that nourishes health and keeps you from sinking into an abyss. Find your lifeline that pulls you from anguish. Say it again and again. Pain is inevitable; suffering is optional.

> *Pain is inevitable; suffering is optional.*

Tanya's pain-free body did not have the stimulus to call her body's defense plan into action. She needed the gift of pain. Maybe the very thing that seems to be the hardship of your life will be the significant gift that enriches your every moment. Sometimes losing something we want helps us find what we actually need. All sunshine and no rain is a desert—not a blessing.

Difficulties put you on a train that seems to be speeding recklessly down the track. That isn't the time to throw away your ticket and jump off. Just sit still and trust the engineer. In time you may find your journey will take you to places of unexpected blessings.

Let's meet the emotions that try to keep us captive as we journey through life. They are gremlins intent on holding us hostage to what cannot be changed. Appreciating their power emboldens us to fight through their webs that imprison our thoughts and make us feel unable.

LIFELINES

1. If you do not feel pain when things are askew, you will not be healthy in body, mind, or spirit.

2. The body heals automatically; the emotions heal by conscious choice.

3. What we think is as important to our spirit as what we eat is to our body.

4. Being locked in emotional pain opens a Pandora's box of ill health.

5. Gratitude to God is the single most important controllable response that nourishes health.

6. Sometimes losing something we want helps us find what we actually need.

7. It is not our recognition of pain but rather our response to it that determines our journey.

8. Pain is inevitable; suffering is optional.

9. All sunshine and no rain is a desert—not a blessing.

5

Redirecting Your Thoughts and Your Emotions

Control the direction of your thoughts and you control the direction of your life.

■ ANCHOR: I counter negative thoughts through gratitude for the gifts in my life, including the lessons I learn from coping with a calamity.

Dr. Caroline Leaf, a neuroscientist and author of several books on the brain's chemistry, states that the number one rule for good physical and mental health is positive thinking, even in the midst of calamity. How is it possible to follow such counsel when your marriage dissolves, your job is cut, or your child is on drugs? How is one to "grin and bear it" when on chemo? Is it realistic to be cheery when you can barely get out of bed? Doesn't longing for what is no more show you cared?

Thoughts and emotions go together like a hand and a glove. What we think is what we feel, and in times of crisis both thoughts and emotions are fear-filled and anxious. To be positive in such times would be a sure sign we were reading life unrealistically. Regardless, Dr. Leaf is right that science is proving the injunction written in Scripture that "whatever is true, whatever is noble, whatever is right, whatever is pure, whatever is lovely, whatever is admirable—if anything is excellent or praiseworthy—think about such things."[1]

The statistics prove that the more we focus on the hopelessness or injustice of our situation, the more toxic hormones and chemicals are activated by the stress. These chemical changes erode our physical and mental health. By being grateful for the little things in the midst of problems, we prevent feelings of anger, fear, or guilt from spewing poison that puts our health in jeopardy. A positive focus is like premium gas in a car, helping our body systems run smoothly even when under tremendous stress.

Look at a few of the statistics on the effect of emotions on our health:

- More than 1,400 known physical and chemical responses and thirty different hormones are activated in response to negative or positive emotions.[2]
- T-cell production critical to the immune system decreases in response to stress.
- A whopping 60–75 percent of the illnesses that plague us, such as cancers, asthma, skin problems, and allergies, just to name a few, are a direct result of stress.[3]
- There are six times more strokes, four times more heart attacks, or ten times more psychosomatic disorders such as

ulcers, hypertension, respiratory ailments, and gastrointestinal problems within the first two years after an emotional or physical crisis.[4]

- Sexual dysfunction is common.[5]

Changing from an inevitable nosedive when problems seem insurmountable to recognizing problems as opportunities protects the body, mind, and spirit. We need to find our way to positive thoughts, for that is the key to healing the body and spirit. Focusing on good makes our body healthier, our mind clearer, our thoughts more optimistic, and our spirit lighter and more enthusiastic.

I tried to focus on the good in life when LeeAnne died, but my thoughts swirled around wanting her presence. I swam laps, walked for miles, and cleaned our woods—physical acts to tire my body. I wore headphones to listen to lectures. I focused on the needs of my family and community. At night, when the quiet settled and my thoughts ran rampant, I watched movies until my squirrelly mind tired. (My brain was too foggy to read.) I refused to allow the constant play of longing thoughts, yet I could not stop the vermin from crawling into my mind, regardless of my effort or prayers. Is that true for you? It is *not* possible to stop your thoughts from pulling to the hurts when you are in crisis. However, it *is* possible to refuse to wallow in those negative thoughts!

Two years after LeeAnne's death, I was diagnosed with a potential brain tumor. I went in for a CT scan, thinking that if my life were over, so be it. Be assured that thought passes through many minds when it seems easier to be released to a better life than to continue struggling through this one. I hope that is not a thought in your mind, but if so, even though it is often a part of dealing with catastrophe, there is a better answer and a way to let go of the consuming ache that fills your spirit. There are lifelines and anchors.

The scan showed a stroke, etiology unknown. I was a classic example of the effect of stress on health. I needed mind control. I needed to turn longing into gratitude. I needed to be grateful for the time I had shared a precious child's life, for the strength I saw in her to be happy in a weak body, for a family that bonded rather than collapsed. Prayer, doing, and time help but they are not the key. It is one's choice to find the diamond in the coal that quiets the raging emotions that cause health crises.

> It is one's choice to find the diamond in the coal that quiets the raging emotions.

CaringBridge, an internet media outlet that allows those in a health crisis to journal their personal stories to encourage support and prayer, shared the story of the family of ten-year-old Brody, who limped to the car after a soccer game. Brody's parents, thinking he had a torn ligament or a minor sprain, sought help in an emergency room. After multiple scans the diagnosis was cancer of the bone. Within days the child went from soccer to chemo to leg amputation. The family was stunned.

Each day they tried to see some evidence of good in their drama—a call, a kindness, a door that opened. They wanted to focus on the little, special things so they would not miss God's blessings in the midst of their challenges. One story shared was of a beautiful young hairdresser who volunteered to cut Brody's hair short so it would be less traumatic when his hair fell out. As she cut his hair she complimented him on his good looks and told of handsome basketball players who buzzed their hair. The family's focus on the surprises and kindness of others has kept hope alive. Their positive outlook and stalwart stance in the midst of a crisis is an example of faith in action.

The difficulty is that serious problems do not resolve themselves overnight. People tire. Friends pull away to problems in their own life. Emotions scream. This wise couple sought advice as to what to expect so they could keep their emotions from simmering toxins into a deadly brew as they worked with the compiling issues. They recognized that shock makes it possible to survive the first period of time after a catastrophe. Shock enables us to ask for help and work toward a goal, one step at a time. This family wanted to look further than the immediate challenges. But how?

Emotions in Balance

The good news is that new research clearly shows the tremendous amount of control our thoughts have over our physical and mental health. We can deflect our thoughts at any time before, during, or after we find ourselves locking into our hurt. Positive thoughts can help the amazing mind restructure new pathways in as little as twenty-one days. Does this mean you will never have thoughts that threaten to pull you down? Of course not! If a pathway has become an expressway, you won't be rid of its control in three weeks, but you can lessen its power. If added to your problem is addiction to a substance, physical cravings are also part of the muddle. Still, though you can't stop a thought from knocking or a substance-need from begging at your mind's door, you don't have to invite them in to stay.

It is difficult to keep emotions in balance in times of challenge. No one wants zombielike emotions, flat and unresponsive. Positive emotions enable us to feel excited about new opportunities so that we take chances, weep when we are hurt, and make sacrifices because we care. We jump for joy when a goal is achieved or sing out when we are in love. Most of us do not indulge the negative emotions like stress or anger that spin off our little daily encounters. They are insignificant gnats, bothersome but easy to shoo away.

But when we experience unjust or disheartening problems, it is in our DNA to lose it! Experiments with multiple species of animals show the animal that judges its treat or treatment to be overtly unfair throws a tantrum. Though strong reactions to unfairness may be normal for the animal kingdom, of which we are a part, expressing emotion vehemently in our culture is considered out of control. How are we to control our nature in times of chaos when emotions go haywire? It is as if they are on steroids—overly intense, spastic, consuming, and out of control!

For intense emotions, we have three options:

- We can *implode* (stuff it down, avoid it, or pretend it is not there).
- We can *explode* (blast it out disrespectfully or destructively).
- We can *recognize*, *appreciate*, and *use* the emotion appropriately.

The problem is that imploding and exploding are easy responses to emotional drama. Recognizing, appreciating, or appropriately expressing our emotions is difficult. Professionals advise that we should feel our emotions and then express our feelings in appropriate ways—*this is the pits; it hurts*—and, finally, resolutely determine our course. Our understanding and our methods of assuaging our pain complicate the healing process. Unlike the pantyhose ad that says one size fits all, when it comes to emotions what seems right for one can be wrong for another. We read from different manuals.

You can't stop a thought from knocking at your mind's door, but you don't have to invite it in to stay.

It is especially difficult if we were not taught healthy ways to cope with feelings that are intense and discombobulating. Just look at children. They are present in the moment and let you know exactly what they feel—and then off they go in peace if their crisis was acknowledged and validated. If they are told to stifle their emotions or that it is wrong to express them, they become confused, questioning and hiding what they feel or acting out to demand attention. Their understanding becomes twisted.

A positive or negative outlook can be trained to become your enduring focus. Conscious mental training such as prayer, study of materials of faith, and reflection stimulate and energize you. Being grateful for the little things in the midst of handling the big ones, like the family on CaringBridge, helps you trust good can come from such bad. Deflection of self-centered focus helps you become more empathetic and sensitive. You recognize everyone has issues with which they struggle. Personal problems seem less devastating. Enthusiasm and a sense of well-being imbed in your spirit.

The question is *how*. Though our mind is programmed to return to "happy" after a crisis, it appears we must affirm that process through our directed thoughts. You must:

- Face the reality realistically, not glossing over wrongs or denying the difficulty of such a life change.
- Admit it is difficult!
- Speak truthfully to yourself—*this is the pits; it hurts!*
- Determine that the crisis will not consume or destroy you.
- Develop your plan to resolve the issue or find ways to live with it.
- Turn your thoughts from what you *don't* have to what you *do* have.
- Use positive trigger thoughts to keep negative thoughts under control.

Trigger Thoughts

I have often observed physicians counseling patients who are in a state of panic about their health. A caring physician will try to calm the patient's concerns by explaining that the patient's feelings of concern are legitimate. He or she assures the patient that it is normal in crisis to feel the care is inadequate, the treatments are unhelpful, and the plan is not working. The physician then tries to partner with the patient to address his or her concerns and establish an acceptable plan.

A doctor was talking with a patient in critical care. The patient felt he was dying. The doctor confirmed that he might die. On the other hand, the doctor continued, with care the patient might not die so soon. The doctor then suggested that if he were dying, the patient needed to enjoy the moments he had, share his thoughts and appreciation with those he loved, and trust his belief that he would transition to another life. He said he could give the patient no guarantees except that panic would not help his situation.

He then continued, "I hope you are going to be able to leave this hospital. For now, fill your mind with something positive. When you are at home, seek ways to keep your thoughts from swirling around your health problems—enjoy a hobby, read a book, watch a movie, talk with family and friends, plan a vacation. The goal is to keep busy, so your thoughts do not dance around your ills."

Using thoughts to change negative feelings is critical to countering their pull as we journey through our travail. We must stop the negative thoughts that cause fear, hopelessness, and panic. Triggers are quick thoughts that reverse our focus, engendering swirling emotions. They keep the difficulties from becoming life locks. Thoughts like *I can't . . . I'll never survive . . . I will never forgive* simply cause our spirit to die. Zest flees. Enthusiasm plummets. Hopelessness reigns.

Find your trigger to counter each life lock that bounces into your consciousness and begs you to give up. The trigger must address the hurt and be repeated with sincerity until the power of the negative thought is gone. "Gone" is temporary; until you counter the hurt, repeatedly, it will keep rearing its ugly head. Use your trigger each time a negative thought arises and its power will weaken over time.

Let's look at a few examples of using a trigger thought to turn a devastating negative thought into a sense of gratitude for the experience.

- Death of a loved one. *I am so glad it hurts because it means my relationship was significant.*
- Ill health. *I am so grateful I was healthy. This pain helps me appreciate how someone else who suffered was so heroic.*
- Longing. *I understand the struggle of others who are longing.*
- Broken relationship. *I am glad I am able to make a commitment even though others are unable to do so. I learned so much about what is good and what is not in a relationship.*
- Abusive relationships. *I learned what I do not want in a relationship. I learned how I will treat others with whom I am in relationship.*
- Loss of a job. *I honed my skill and am ready for my next venture.*

Focusing on the positive in no way keeps you from seeking justice for wrongs. It simply keeps you from being tied to revenge. It does not force you to forget someone you love; instead, memories comfort rather than provoke tears. Once you feel the freedom from bondage to a negative focus, you will refuse to be captive again to experiences, wrongs, or losses that drag you into darkness. (We will discuss the power of trigger thoughts again in chapter 9, "The Stories You Believe.")

In times of trials and suffering, strong emotions make us deeply uncomfortable and unhappy. It is in such moments, propelled by our distress, that those who overcome determine to focus on the flower amid the weeds. Author Suzanne Woods Fisher shares the tragedy of holding on to the hurts of life:

> When we nurse grudges, hold on to hurts, let anger fester, allow resentments and bitterness to brew—things that foul our life and spoil relationships, we do with our memories, emotions and relationships what we wouldn't do with rotten bananas and spoiled milk. We refuse to let go of the garbage.[6]

But how do we keep our thoughts and emotions from turning our experiences into garbage? Certainly we must rid ourselves of the *anger* and *guilt* that swell in difficult times.

LIFELINES

1. Emotions will follow actions.
2. It is our choice to find the diamond in the coal that quiets the raging emotions.
3. After crisis we are programmed to return to "happy," but it appears we must affirm that process through our directed thoughts.
4. We must turn our thoughts from what we *don't* have to what we *do* have.
5. Well-being depends upon our being present in reality and at peace with where we are.
6. We can redirect our thoughts at any time before, during, or after we find ourselves consumed by loss, injustice, or immoral or wrong actions.

6

Handling the Bully

Stewing may soften meat but it hardens the heart.

■ **ANCHOR: I respect anger, use it carefully, and shake it off!**

Let's just face it. In many situations anger is a good thing, our first responder—our discerning alarm that something is wrong, attacking our safety, and upsetting our equilibrium. It is a tool to help us analyze what to do, what to avoid, and how to seek justice. Anger alerts us to danger. That is its good face.

But anger has another side. It is an addiction that swallows joy, indwells pessimism, and throws suspicion. Especially in times of trauma, anger seeks residence in one's spirit. Left to simmer, its insidious nature keeps emotions on edge. It is a bully that pushes for control. It must be put back in its sentinel post to fulfill its duty of warning us of danger or it will morph into a terrorist that blows our world apart.

Following crisis, anger hangs back as shock, numbness, denial, and grace show up. Shock is there when the doctor tells you the biopsy was positive for cancer. You don't remember another thing he said. Numbness arrives as you read your wife's note that she wants a divorce. Didn't you read it repeatedly to get your head around the words? Grace supported Paul and me as we left the hospital after our six-year-old daughter LeeAnne's death. We thanked people for sharing their condolences, mouthed clichés, and held back the tears. Denial joined us after our adult daughter Kim's death when our ten-year-old grandson, Michael, put his arm around me and said, "We are going to be okay, Bebe. We are strong," echoing the words of his mother as she fought leukemia. Anger builds slowly after the foursome—shock, numbness, denial, and grace—go to bed.

> *Anger builds slowly after the foursome—shock, numbness, denial, and grace— go to bed.*

Anticipate anger, for in difficult times patience is AWOL, absent without leave. Emotions are simmering. Stress depletes our reserve of "niceness" so it feels fair to strike at those in our safety zone—family, friends, or complete strangers. John recalled anger's rush after he lost his job and his son discovered, when signing up for his semester courses in his junior year of college, that a prerequisite course's professor had resigned. Without that course three hundred students would need to wait until another professor was hired, adding an additional year of college to their program. John called the dean of the business school, who was gracious but said there was simply nothing he could do. John felt as if someone put a hot poker on his foot. He felt scalding hot from the bottom of his feet to the top of his head. He blurted out, "Nothing?!" His anger felt out of bounds.

John did not think his anger felt rational, but we agreed it was *normal*. The course problem had *nothing* to do with his job loss, but his rage had *everything* to do with it. It was another out-of-control situation in a time when his reserves were already drained. The problem is that John, like too many of us, was taught *never* to be angry; instead, we should all learn *how* to be angry.

Anger is crucial! It is a needed part of our healthy emotions—but it is one letter short of danger. Crisis makes it particularly volatile. Expect anger when life is askew. It sneaks in the back door. Remember when your emotions were simmering? Did a verbal bomb suddenly come out of your mouth? Did you justify your short fuse by such comments as *He made me angry . . . She burns me up . . . They always . . .* That is not acceptable because anger will burn bridges, ruin relationships, and eat your health and sense of well-being. Marriages die under the strain, children flee home, employees walk out, and violence increases.

Mark Twain is attributed as saying, "Anger is an acid that can do more harm to the vessel in which it is stored than to anything on which it is poured." So true; anger is damaging to the person who allows it residence. Anger:

is highly volatile,

can explode like a bombshell,

may implode, pulling you into depression and guilt,

is quick to respond when one's buttons are frayed,

thrives on its rightness,

festers and stacks blame,

assigns culpability,

is a minefield that raises up retaliation and rage,

can set us at odds with anything and everyone, and

is driven by fears, insecurity, and/or self-defensiveness.

Research shows that even one five-minute episode of anger is so stressful it can impair your immune system by lowering T-cell production and can decrease, for more than six hours, levels of serotonin, dopamine, and melatonin—the hormones that affect happiness. Prolonged bouts of anger or guilt take a toll on the body, causing high blood pressure, anxiety, headaches, poor circulation, heart attacks, and strokes, as well as providing a breeding ground for leukemia and cancers. Just listing the problems makes me want to avoid anger and its twin emotion, guilt. They, like arsenic, are dangerous toxins. But though we can't steer clear of either—and to do so would be a sure indication of a lack of self-esteem and an inability to correctly view experiences that are potentially hurtful—we can learn to use these emotions as they are intended.

Too many of us have been taught never to be angry; instead we should have learned how to be angry.

Anger is destructive when it controls you. It is constructive when it is used to alert you to a problem. It's a lot like money in your hand. Hold the money tight and it is of no value. Throw it carelessly away and it is of no value. Money is only valuable if it is used with discretion. Likewise, the goal of anger management is to use your anger productively.

Handling the Bully

Be aware that anger seeks a punching bag. And who reaps the anger more than anyone else—those closest to the angry bird! Your teen is unhappy. Who does she blame? Mom or Dad. A child dies, and within two years more than half of couples divorce. Your adult child is unhappy in his marriage so he faults his upbringing. The target needs no reality-based justification. "I couldn't stand being with 'happy' people!" commented a young woman. Her stressful job caused her uncontrolled anger to add to her anxiety. She spun off anger at anyone whose attitude was optimistic or demeanor was cheerful. Uncontrolled anger:

causes anxiety,

drives emotions toward others to be irrationally hot or icy cold,

targets others, regardless of their involvement in the issue,

makes one feel out of control, and

causes irrational fear.

Consider these suggestions when you are dealing with difficulties brought on by anger.

Acknowledge your anger.

Instead of pushing your anger into the recesses of your mind or refusing to admit it is there, be mindful of what you are feeling. Look deep within yourself and ask why you are upset. If you can admit that you are angry, you can tackle the emotions and find a resolution to the problem. If you allow anger to morph into rage, stop. Take a deep breath and pause. Think through a plan that will prevent actions you will regret later.

Calm down before you address the issue.

You need calm to consider your action's long-term effect. You may stop an immediate storm but create a hurricane if you tackle a difficult emotional issue before you are self-controlled. Pray before you speak. Studies in England found that people who prayed were able to handle stressful situations with more calm. Prayer is a balm to an offended spirit.

Be reasonable and caring.

The only hope for turning away anger is sincere, kindly expressed care. That requires diplomacy and respect. Ask any parent of a child using drugs, experiencing diet issues, cutting, failing in school, and the like, and they will assure you that force or incentives may work for a little while but ultimately the course of action is chosen by the individual. If you are dealing with an issue that is driving your fears for the safety or well-being of someone about whom you care—or even yourself—share your thoughts and concerns. Affirm that you believe the individual wants to make wise choices—or that it is possible to do the "whatever." Your best chance of winning an argument or finding a compromise is to let the person know you are not against him or her as you seek a resolution to the problem together.

A father offered his advice after dealing with a son who struggled with addiction. "It isn't possible to understand why someone you care about does something that messes up his or her life. I was ballistic with my brilliant son who messed up his life on drugs. I paid for rehab, bailed him out of jail, begged, rewarded, the whole gamut. Ultimately, I resolved that my anger did no good—and it was ruining me! His sedative was a bad choice that only he could stop. It was sad, but anger was my vice and no help to him."

When you confront someone who is armed and ready to fight, speak with respect and hope. Asking is often better than telling. For example, "Could I help? What would you like? Do you think it would be helpful to find a good counselor, rehab program, take a vacation, hire a helping hand . . . ?" Ushering dictums or words that imply failure, such as "You need to get help," or "I can't handle your . . ." is a death knell for any suggestion.

Be careful when you try to protect yourself or someone else.

You do not want to make a bad situation worse. Good help might be the wrong help, so consider carefully the boomerang possibility. You are responsible for the way you handle your anger but also for how you handle the anger of others.

I was at a T-ball game where a raging mother with two small children sat in front of me. The mother was seriously out of control and the children's fear was palpable. I needed to help but at the same time be aware that doing help the wrong way might jeopardize the children's safety. A confronted mother, frustrated by a criticism, might rage at home. I sat down beside the mother and put my arm around the younger child. "Friend," I said to the mother, "you are a trooper. It is tough trying to handle little wiggle worms. Would you allow me to get you a soft drink and maybe a snack for the kids while I get a Coke? A snack helped my children be still at these long games."

Obviously, this mother came to the game to sit on the hard stands in the heat with young children to support her six-year-old son. She brought her children when someone else might leave her little ones home unattended. I bore responsibility if my actions caused the mother to be more aggressive when she was not in a public situation. The mother needed major parent training so that she could care properly for her family—but not at that moment.

Don't do something stupid.

Some of us are facing critical issues with someone in our circle of family or friends. Offer help and give encouragement, but if the situation is not ours to manage *don't let your mouth get ahead of your brain.* Anger can cause us to do and say things that scuttle any hope of our influencing the situation. We end up beating ourselves up when we see the result of our actions, asking, *What was I thinking?*

> When in confrontation, do not let your mouth get ahead of your brain.

I spoke to a man who was in a difficult relationship with a screwed-up person in his extended family. He shared a great insight. "For years I spun around her irregular behavior until a lightbulb turned on in my head. Who was messed up? Obviously I was allowing someone to light my fuse and set me on fire. My actions did not change the loony tune but they certainly changed me—and not for the good!"

Focus on what you can do to solve the problem without a heated exchange.

In the heat of the moment, throwing in issues from the past is unfair but easy to do. References such as "You always do" or "You did" are like gasoline to flaming emotions. *It is inevitable that an explosion follows or hope deadens.* Sometimes agreeing to disagree is the only resolution. There are arguments that will never be won. Diplomacy knows when to let something go.

Seek help.

You need help if you are getting into trouble with your co-workers, your friends and family, or even the law. There are many therapists, classes, and programs for anger management problems. Asking for help is not a sign of weakness; it is a sign of strength. It is a decision to live a more peaceful and content life. Knowing when what you feel is normal—or is out of balance—gives you a guideline.

Use Common Sense

The reason you grow angry when you are dealing with difficulties is that you care. And when you care it is difficult to be kind and tactful if you perceive the world to be collapsing. Still, you must try. Your actions will either create hostility and irreparable rifts or soften anger and build trust. Get a grip. Being angry, sarcastic, kidding with jabs, or refusing to talk through a problem puts daggers in the heart of a relationship. Rebuilding a broken relationship is possible if you refuse to be negative, refuse to retort, and always suggest there is hope. No one responds well to control or feeling stabbed by words and gestures.

There are some basic techniques that take the oomph out of anger:

- Relax. Tension elevates stress and negative reactive behavior.
- Before stressful times, listen to uplifting music, focus on something positive, or exercise to increase your endorphins.
- Know your goal.
- Recognize you cannot force change.
- Be intentional to do what is right, regardless of what someone else does.
- Be careful of your presentation of the issue that stirs your anger.
- Pull away from the negative situation or person until you are able to control your words and actions.
- Apologize when you lose control of your actions and words.
- Repeatedly say statements that reflect hope. "I know we can work through this problem," "I want to help you," "I love you," "I hear what you are saying," and "Could we try . . ." are all a good place to begin.
- Recognize that the person who loses his or her cool also loses the argument.

The reason you grow angry is because you care.

I might have made it through our loss without my husband, but struggling through it with him has strengthened our bond. We both had many times we had to back up and change course. I hope you are mustering through the tough times that injustices and losses cause in your significant relationships. But if not, forgive yourself, learn, and move on. Regardless of your situation, you have only two choices: respecting your anger, using it, and then moving on, or stewing in the brew. It is true that life is too short to be angry and hold a grudge—and it is also too long!

LIFELINES

1. We have only two choices in dealing with anger: hold on and stew, or use it and let it go.
2. The reason you grow angry is because you care.
3. Don't let your mouth get ahead of your brain when angry.
4. You may not be able to change a particular person or situation but you can control your response to both.
5. Winning an argument is not as important as growing a caring relationship built on mutual respect.
6. Diplomacy knows when to let something go.
7. If your relationship is in trouble, get a grip.

The Elephant in the Room

The only mistake you ever truly make is the mistake you never learn from.

■ ANCHOR: I face my guilt, own it, make amends, and learn from it.

Guilt is my plague. It fills my thoughts during the day and wakes me at night. It floats me in regret. If only I had . . . Why did I? I'm sorry for what I did, sorry for what I didn't do, sorry there wasn't more time. I'm sorry that I didn't understand, that I missed opportunities, that I couldn't stop the inevitable. Guilt plays endless tunes of what if and I wish. What if I had done differently? I wish I could go back to do it over. I failed.

Guilt always partners with trouble. It feels like a demon on your back eating away at your spirit. It demands you face the issues that belong to you. It causes you to question your actions, prioritize, and choose your path. If you face the issues guilt brings to the surface, discern their legitimacy, own the ones that are yours, make amends, and let them go, then guilt becomes a gift. It offers you an opportunity to right your priorities, face your wrongs, and accept responsibility for your life. It humbles your pride. It forces you to deal with ownership and take responsibility for your actions. Acknowledged, lessons are learned and hope blossoms. Regret changes to compassion.

Guilt nags mercilessly if you hide from it or fail to address the issues. It morphs into shame. Shame shapes one's core. It causes you to feel dirty and unworthy. It defines you as stuck, the situation unchangeable. You believe the lies that spin off its ferocity: *I can't do anything right . . . I'm not worth anything . . . I'm a failure . . . I can't break my addiction to . . . I can't leave this abusive relationship . . . I can't be happy.* It fills you with regret. Regret is painful. You hide or bully.

In 1970 a Boston bank robbery by the Black Panthers, a group of college students who protested against the Vietnam War, went terribly wrong. Boston police officer Walter Schroeder was shot multiple times during the heist. A line of his brothers in the police force stretched around St. Mary's Hospital as they queued to give over three hundred pints of blood for Schroeder. My husband was one of the physicians who tried diligently to stop Sgt. Schroeder's bleeding, but it couldn't be stopped and he died. Six of the co-conspirators were arrested, but one, Katherine Ann Power, got away.

Power changed her identity to Alice Metzinger, obtained a birth certificate and social security number, and spent two decades working and raising a family in Oregon. She taught cooking classes in a college, was a consultant for a tea and coffee shop, and became a partner in a New York restaurant and bakery. When her only child was fourteen, after twenty-three years in hiding, Power turned herself in to the police. She told the truth, apologized to the Schroeder family, pled guilty, and was imprisoned for six years. Released, she declared that the more difficult prison was not the one with iron bars; it was the one in her head that was awash in guilt.

Linda Caroll, a therapist, described the change in Katherine's demeanor after the confession, trial, and prison as remarkable. It was almost impossible to envision the bespectacled cook as one of the Federal Bureau of Investigation's ten most wanted fugitives, a violent activist, and jailbird. People questioned why she confessed, trading her family, career, and friends for a jail cell. Her answer: *guilt was rotting her insides*. Guilt slept with her and awakened with her. She carried it throughout the day. Her confession and imprisonment set her free.

It wasn't just Sgt. Schroeder's life that was affected by the robbery. He had a wife and nine kids who after his death were raised in public housing. There was no way Katherine Power's jail time or probation could make up for their loss of a father and husband. The sad life experiences of the Schroeder family will either strengthen or cripple them. In all of life's challenges each of us must choose to overcome or to wear the cloak of victimhood.

Send the Elephant on Its Way

Guilt is tenacious. It demands one accept responsibility for his or her actions. No tiptoeing around, pretending an untruth. No justifying a wrong. No excuses or blame games. Guilt floods us like the Mississippi River. So one of the first things you need to do when you are dealing with your tsunami is make peace with your guilt.

The good news is that guilt belongs to the guilty. That makes guilt easier to deal with than anger. Whatever belongs to you is under your control. Guilt asks you to act responsibly and nags until you do. To rid yourself of guilt's grip you must follow its dictum: face the truth, own your mistakes, make amends if possible, and learn. If you deal truthfully and work through the issues guilt brings to the surface, your slate is cleaned and your sense of self-worth is reset.

Guilt tears us down if it morphs into shame, making us feel dirty and unworthy.

A mother shared her story of guilt. Both of her sons had died. She said the son who died first was her *good* son, the one in medical school. The mother was grieving, idealizing the deceased child, when the *bad* son did something wrong that triggered words buried in her heart: "It should have been you!" The young man nodded. "You are right, Mom. It should have been me." Hours later the police awakened her with news the youth was found dead from a self-inflicted wound. Guilt plowed into her heart. Regret took up residence.

There are words that can't be taken back and acts that can't be undone. That mother can never undo the tragedy her words spurred nor eradicate her pain from such loss. But flailing herself to erase the guilt will never ease her anguish. The mother must find her way back to peace in the same way as anyone who wishes he or she could turn back the clock, take back the words, or redo the past.

Guilt points squarely at the person who owns the wrong. It forces us to deal with ownership and responsibility for our actions. Acknowledging it, we can learn from the past and fill the present with hope. Regret changes to compassion.

> **Guilt**
>
> Face it.
> Own it.
> Make amends if possible.
> Learn from your mistakes.

Katherine Power determined she needed to accept the social punishment for her involvement in a crime and to apologize to the family of the fallen hero. It did not free her from her responsibility for the wrong, nor did it make her a heroine for doing the right thing. It did put a boot to the elephant that sat with her night and day for all those years. Sometimes the weight we carry has far more to do with our failures than the pounds on our body.

The fact that you are saddened by your wrongs is a good sign that you are not a narcissist, a paranoid personality, or a psychopath. Those with such personalities go on a counterattack, becoming outraged at being humiliated or embarrassed when their motives are suspect. However, wearing guilt like a mantle is as damaging as refusing to be honest about your wrong.

Many of us have a good share of serious pain from failed relationships, too much food or alcohol, not enough time for our kids, our failures, and the endless list goes on. We layer ourselves with walls to keep guilt from dominating our thoughts but it creeps in, causing us to feel sneaky or filled with self-loathing like Katherine Power. Freedom requires we acknowledge our wrong and learn from it. Suppressed feelings cause abscesses in the soul. It is better to come clean than to slowly rot.

> *The weight we carry may have far more to do with our losses and failures than the pounds on our body.*

Pride wants to hide imperfection. No one ever choked to death from swallowing their pride but many have lost their sense of peace because they failed to put pride aside. You may have justified your wrong actions or attitude by one of the four coverall excuses that all begin with "I" and are self-centered, self-concerned, and self-focused!

- I deserve to retaliate.
- I deserve to get it.
- I am afraid of rejection, criticism, failure if I . . .
- I don't want to.

Mending a Wound

It is tough to get past pride. It is painful to accept responsibility for an offense. Still, if the issue stings it is because *you care*; otherwise you would brush off hurtful words and actions as if they were gnats. Guilt hiding in regret requires that you attend to the issue so you can be free from a festering wound. Healing a broken relationship requires an apology or the relationship becomes permanently damaged, just as physical wounds need to be attended to in order to prevent infection's spread.

It's better to come clean than to slowly rot from the inside out.

You may feel only a tiny bit responsible for a conflict, but you need to apologize for that bit. A free spirit requires that you follow this rule: apologize to whomever you hurt, directly, succinctly, and most of all sincerely. This doesn't mean you must continue the relationship. Instead, it frees you from guilt for *your* wrongs so you can continue on your journey without baggage. Your goal is a free spirit. That isn't possible without letting go of the hurts and anger embodied in a bad start, sad years, and hard times.

Handling Guilt

No one is perfect; no relationship is flawless. We all have reason to harbor the little worm of guilt that eats our zeal for life. It took Katherine Power twenty-three years to oust her guilt. I determined when our daughter Kim died that I had truly done my best to meet her needs, so instead of burying myself in all the ways I might have been a better mother, I chose to believe she knew that I loved her more than my own life and now looks down from above to wish us well.

Steps to Releasing Guilt

Recognize your responsibility for the wrong.
Throw away justifications.
Confess it.
Try to make amends.
Use the experience as a learning tool.
Change.

Guilt rides a mighty mount. If you struggle with guilt, putting it on like a coat and feeling less than perfect, get over it! Don't allow your pride to keep you in bondage. Humility unties the bindings that tie you to image and perfection. Try these positive ways to reflect on the changes guilt demands.

1. **Take time away.** You are more able to reflect on resolution of your guilt if you are not trying to squeeze reflection into a busy schedule.

2. **Seek the truth.** The question is simple: Did you do wrong? Be sorrowful for the failures, rid yourself of pity parties, and determine a better way.

3. **Refuse blame that does not belong to you.** Accept responsibility for what you are responsible for—nothing else.

4. **Talk to someone about what's on your mind.** Consider carefully with whom you share your guilt—the one you have wronged, a friend, or a professional. Confessions are not to justify your wrong or give the aura of humility. Confess to deal with your sincere regret for a wrong. Your goal is to change behavior that harms your self-esteem and relationships.

5. **Don't ruminate over your wrong.** You cannot erase the past. Wallowing in sorrow for your wrongs causes a multitude of

unhealthy coping mechanisms. Figure out what you can do to quit spinning around your bondage to guilt.

6. **Be wary of broadcasting your guilt.** Stay away from venting your guilty feelings to friends and family. The words once spoken, emailed, texted, or mailed cannot be taken back.

The Art of Apologies

A good apology is an art. Is it easy? Of course not! Humbling yourself is one of life's most difficult ventures. Person to person is always the best way to apologize. Written apologies are an absolute no for the difficult stuff. Cards are dubious even if the issue is minor. Admittedly, some cards seem an easy shortcut and lessen the fear of more confrontation. Telephone calls are missing an important ingredient—facial expression. People read sincerity more than they hear it. If you want to hug and make up, make it personal. The best hugs are when you wrap your arms around the individual, figuratively, and apologize for your words or actions.

Suggestions for Apologizing

- Choose a neutral place where you can talk privately, honestly, and openly.
- Start with your goal imbedded in your mind—a peace treaty, not a battle to win your point.
- Recognize the importance of body language. People need to *see* sincerity.
- Simply state your goal: *I want peace. I am sorry. I have limits.*
- Listen respectfully without trying to correct minutia or their interpretation of the issue.
- Stick to the issue.

- Avoid the small stuff.
- State your feelings: *I care. I need . . .*
- Express sincere appreciation of their stated feelings: *Thank you for letting me know . . . I am sorry you felt that . . .*
- Try to correct misunderstandings: *I'm sorry, that is not what I meant to convey.*
- Absolutely, offer no excuses for your failure or wrong.
- Apologize for your wrongdoing, not your thoughts.

Most of us come to a time of apology with our guns loaded, waiting for the other party to apologize. Defenses are on high alert. If you want to mend the rift or take responsibility for a wrong, let go of your excuses. Refuse to take offense. Many apologies end up escalating a war.

Some apologies are fruitless; some are insincere. Sincere apologies aren't given out like popcorn or used as a blanket to cover all and invoke an aura of humility. Nor are they like some in politics—who get caught, lie, and then fess up under the pressure. An apology must not be a tell-all session or a search for absolution. It is not appropriate to apologize for the actions of someone else, even though you may express your sorrow for someone else's actions. Do not apologize for expressing anger if you are countering another who has trampled on the boundaries of decency, safety, and respect. A sincere apology is an acknowledgment of your responsibility for your wrong, not your thoughts.

There are three classic examples of an apology done wrong! One, a company executive apologized to a staff member for his thoughts of lust for her. What was his purpose—to show his righteousness, to blame her for his feelings, or perhaps to draw her into fulfilling his desire? Two, President Clinton's hand-in-the-cookie-jar apology for his affair with Monica Lewinsky. He was sorry for being "caught." Three, Bill McCartney, the founder of Promise

Keepers, apologized for his one-night affair before an audience of thousands at a national, televised conference. His unsuspecting wife was stunned. The apology sounded like adrenaline-driven false humility.

If you have blown it, said something you regret, growled when you should have smiled, or simply done wrong, remember that the most difficult seven words to say—"I was wrong. Will you forgive me?"—are also the most healing.

A young man told of meeting with his brother to mend a ten-year rift in their relationship. He was stunned as he listened to his brother's interpretation. It was a gross misread of his actions, but his goal was to mend the relationship, not win the war. He followed the rules of engagement and apologized that his actions had caused hurt. He agreed that his intention of support in a difficult time was obviously not done well. Debate does not heal wounds. Honest apologies do not offer excuses or justifications but do attempt to convey one's intention.

The rule is simple: apologize to whomever you hurt directly, succinctly, and most of all sincerely.

Use the sandwich approach if you need to discuss difficult issues you believe will be perceived as critical or judgmental: say something positive about the person, express your apology as well as your concern, and end the discussion with another positive. We'll talk about this more in chapter 16, "When You Want to Help."

It is often in our forties and fifties that we begin to reflect upon why we harbor guilt. We stop excusing our wrong or hiding who we are. We become aware of how our behavior has affected those in our circle. We apologize for what we have done wrong or failed to do. We do so because we want a new day. We want to begin afresh.

If questions are rising in your spirit, thank God. Your spirit is trying to send the elephant on its way. As soon as you rid yourself of regrets over yesterday that cause heaviness, the twin thieves of anger and guilt will no longer rob you of happiness in the present or hope for the future.

LIFELINES

1. Guilt is a tool that helps us critique what to do, change, or avoid.
2. Guilt asks us to be responsible for our actions and responses.
3. The rule is simple: apologize to whomever you hurt directly, succinctly, and most of all sincerely.
4. The greater tragedy is not the mistake you make but your failure to learn from it.
5. Freedom in your spirit demands you make peace with your guilt.
6. Guilt tears us down if it morphs into shame, making us feel dirty and unworthy.
7. Guilt requires we see the truth—and that when we have done wrong confess it, accept responsibility, and apologize.
8. It is better to come clean than to slowly rot from the inside out.

8

When Problems Stack

Character cannot be developed in ease and quiet.
Only through experience of trial and suffering can
the soul be strengthened, ambition inspired, and
success achieved.

Helen Keller

■ **ANCHOR: I deal with reality—what is changed, what might
be changed, and what will not change.**

No question: you want to handle your life problems with grace.
You are eager to analyze the problem, focus on what you can do,
recognize what you cannot do, and then determine a course of
action to handle the necessary change to resolve the issue. The
problem is that most problems are not simple and do not come
in an orderly fashion, patiently awaiting a solution. They stack.

Honeybees are in a stacking crisis that is threatening our food supply. Honeybees pollinate 80 percent of the plants in the world's food supply, and they are dying in catastrophic numbers. A typical incident in this survival crisis is the death of twenty-five thousand honeybees that fell out of linden trees planted near a Target parking lot in Wilsonville, Oregon. Though pesticides were blamed for the linden tree disaster, the collapse of entire colonies of honeybees is not one fixable problem. Honeybee colony collapse results from multiple factors—parasitic mites, bacteria, nutrition, genetics, habitat loss, weather crisis, pesticides, and two newly found pathogens, a fungus and a virus. How are the scientists and agriculturists to solve this crisis when each problem complicates or generates another problem?

Unfortunately, stacking is always a discombobulating part of crisis. No issue stands alone. Whatever initiates the problem that stuns us is like a magnet that pulls other issues into the fray. Stuffing the issues behind closed doors, denying their existence, or running from them only gives the problem time to become virulent. To handle the cascading problems, actions must be directed toward resolution, problem by problem. Without intentional direction, our reactions spin off emotions that can make a bad situation worse. Tragedy becomes catastrophe. Despair bottoms into hopelessness.

Your goal may be to make a plan and move forward. The problem is that the resolve to move forward is often scuttled by an insignificant side issue. Don't be surprised to find you are swirling around the trivial side issues that attend a crisis. Too often the little, insignificant stuff dims our power to cope with the changes caused by the significant stuff. Your goal to resolve a particular issue or move in a different direction becomes sidetracked by an attention-grabbing problem.

I recognized how easy it is to become sidetracked in my first radio interview after the publication of my book *Sunrise Tomorrow:*

Coping with the Death of a Child. The radio program was to be an hour-long telephone conversation aired live. I hoped to offer tools for recovery and counsel to grieving families and caregivers through the interview.

The problem was that our family had returned from a trip to Disney World the night before the radio program. From Disney World to death is a major shift in focus. A radio interview is best when it's like a talk between friends on the front porch, comfortable and at ease. The questions asked by the host demand quick thinking and clean answers. Pauses in the interview are pregnant. People listening anticipate answers; seconds stretch.

I stayed up most of the night making cheat sheets. If questions were asked about any of the multiple issues, I had quick, perky answers cut from the book and pasted to large construction paper sheets. That morning, after everyone was off to their day's activities, I put a note on our front door, "Do Not Disturb." The house was quiet. Ten minutes until airtime. As I bowed to ask God's insights and calming influence, a fly flew by.

The fly was oblivious to me. He was busy humming, bumping into mirrors and then attacking the windows, back and forth like a kamikaze pilot. I tried to ignore it. I tried to pray through its diving assaults, but when it landed in my hair the quiet was gone. I became centered not on the interview but rather on killing the fly. With a shoe in hand, I leapt over the bed, hit the mirrors, and ran at the fly—without doing anything more than irritating it. I needed a new maneuver, a change of direction. A thought plunged into my panic—open the door and let the fly out of the room. The fly left willingly, leaving me exactly one minute to pull myself together before the phone rang.

Flies in life are everywhere. They are the minor no-see-ums that cause your emotions to rocket and distract you from handling major life issues such as death, financial woes, or disease with grace.[1] The flies in our life:

catch our attention,

become an irritation,

shift our focus,

become a compulsion, and

offer an excuse for failure.

Staying on your plan to overcome and resolve the problems spinning from your calamity demands you not allow the flies of insignificant issues to cause you to swirl. The flies focus us on the irritation of trivialities—what someone did wrong, the negative news, the minor issues. The good news is that, unlike those honeybees, we hold much power to change our situation for the better. Understanding our emotions and recognizing what is normal give us tools to hold us steady when problems compile. We focus best when we center on what "I" can do, rather than on what others should do. Each of us can turn heartbreaking circumstances into a Cinderella story if we begin to look at what is possible rather than long for what is not possible.

Find the Light Switch in the Dark

Change is a constant of life. It is incumbent in crisis. Any change, even change for the better, is accompanied by drawbacks and discomfort. Life is altered. Most of us go through the process of change leaving claw marks behind. We hold on to the past as if it were golden.

A young woman who participated in my seminar on finding joy shared that she became depressed when she moved upward to a better community, more wonderful home, and better schools for her children. She attempted suicide. She had been unprepared for the sense of loss of friends, favorite haunts, and normalcy. She wanted to understand how to adapt more easily. She recognized change is a law of living, and she sought ways to be flexible.

Although it is not possible to anticipate all that will be incumbent in a specific change, it is wise to know what to expect when confronting life-changing circumstances. Many times we are taught what we are *not* supposed to do. I suggested this young woman turn her thinking to *what is okay* in the midst of change. We listed eleven "okays"! Appreciating what is helpful when you are in upheaval helps you feel that though your life is changed, you aren't out of control.

1. It is okay to be emotional.

It is okay to be sad, to grieve, to be angry, or to place blame—at least for a moment. But you can't stay there! Spinning emotions can keep you in a place of helplessness when you need to be in a place of hope and growth.

2. It is okay to talk to someone about your problems.

Let others walk with you on your journey. Give the merely curious a simple statement, "This experience has its ups and downs!" Be open with close friends and professionals. They want to help, not judge. Seek out those who have weathered storms; they have a story to share and lifelines that may help. At the least they can affirm you are not crazy, offer their perspective, or encourage you to seek help.

3. It is okay to ask for help.

Most people are cautious about jumping into the private matters of others, as they should be. Though natural caregivers may be good mind readers, most people stand back until they receive permission to invade your privacy. So when you need help, ask for it. Throw away the language of a two-year-old: "I can do it myself."

4. It is okay to work through your issue as you feel best.

Do not fear advice. It might generate new, helpful thoughts. "Thank you, I will consider that," is a gracious way to reply without committing to something. You will be handling the repercussions of an action, so regardless of someone else's assurance that he or she knows the best course, make sure you are willing to handle the potential fallout.

5. It is okay to seek medical intervention.

Sometimes you may need professional help such as a counselor or a physician. Upheaval may cause physical problems—depletion of chemicals, hormonal shifts, and a multitude of issues that cannot be solved merely by a positive attitude. The body responds to problems with many complex responses that can complicate your problems big-time. It is strength to seek professional help when needed, not weakness.

6. It is okay to feel alone.

Feeling alone is okay, as long as you know it is normal to feel so—but it is also not true. What has happened to you may seem rare, until you begin to look around. We all have our share of difficulties. When our six-year-old daughter died, I knew no one else whose child had died. Yet I can assure you the world is full of grieving parents, and the number of child deaths in the United States goes from two hundred thousand a year upward toward a million, depending on what is counted—miscarriages, age, accidents, disease, and so forth. Be assured there are many with anxieties in life very similar to yours.

7. It is okay to know you will never be the same again.

The ringing question is not if you will change but rather if you will become more caring and compassionate or shrivel inside as you cling to the past. The good news is that the deepest, most stretching, growing, and maturing lessons are born from surviving the problems and catastrophes no one wants. The deepest souls, the wisest people, the kindest and most caring folks are those who have struggled and overcome. The most negative, hateful, spiteful, and venomous individuals are those who, instead of fighting through the emotional pulls, scream "It isn't fair!" and give up.

Accepting change with grace is much more difficult in the short term than just giving up, raging, and blaming. Accepting responsibility for your actions fosters a new maturity. The effort pays off in a big-time wonderful sense of appreciation for every moment of your life. The shift from your losses to your opportunities flows from cultivating a positive outlook. The growth that transpires as you struggle to stand and move forward clears your vision. Insight grows. You become aware of the mysteries of faith. You discern the healing power of gratitude.

8. It is okay to not have it all figured out.

Go slowly! Assuredly problems do not become smaller if you dodge them. However, jumping into action or conclusions too quickly can turn a sandpile of problems into a mountain of woe. Time gives you a chance to calm your emotions and be realistic about potential fallout. Considering your options carefully allows you the opportunity to be wise in a period of unsettling transition. Those who make knee-jerk decisions after a loss or injustice often regret their rashness.

9. It is okay to accept the inevitable.

It is not *resignation* to deal with reality. Clinging to what was but is no more is a surefire way to make your adjustment to change more difficult. You have not forgotten, approved a wrong, or let a culprit off the hook when you decide to move on with life. Instead, you are using discernment to determine what to let go for your sake and sanity.

10. It is okay to trust God and to question Him.

Crisis births more questions than answers. Just be quiet, listen, and keep walking. The answers will come. Vision's hindsight is always clearer when it is no longer blurred by the chaos of change.

11. It is okay to be positive and count your blessings.

Hope keeps our spirit alive and is good for both our physical and mental sides. I know a woman who certainly would treasure her workaholic husband's company but, instead of complaining, declares it a blessing that she has been able to be more independent than many because of his busy schedule; a man who is thankful for his difficult childhood after his mother's death, because it taught him the preciousness of relationships and time; and a child who is blind but feels sorry for those who have sight but no vision. Count your blessings, especially in the worst of circumstances, because *hope born from gratitude* may be your lifeline.

The Gift of Challenge

"I know the horror of stacking problems," claimed a father whose son recently divorced. The divorce was sad for the whole family, almost like a death. It seemed one problem barreled into another. He struggled with which problem to address first. His daughter-in-law wanted reminders of her past behind her and his presence was just that. She warned, "Stay away. We (grandchildren included) don't need you!" The problem was that this father needed all of them. He wanted life like it was—the son content with his marriage, the daughter-in-law finding joy in her role as wife and mother, and the grandchildren growing up in a happy family!

He didn't want change. It is hard to handle your son's or daughter's divorce without taking sides. As the divorce wars escalated, the father/grandfather found himself in the midst of a firing zone. He was realistic and wise. "It was hard to not be anxious, but as bad as this was I have learned a great life lesson. I am responsible for what I do and how I act, not for the actions of others. I am careful to do the right thing. I don't want my actions to make a bad situation worse."

This man realized the only one he could ultimately control or change was himself. He believed the divorce was a tragedy for all involved, so he didn't try to push his agenda or be the know-it-all. Though he ached to voice his needs, he shut his mouth and listened, refusing to be offended. He acted with compassion for all, not just his son. He determined to be an encourager. He openly shared that God loved each person so that each would have hope.

Let's outline how he handled his challenge.

- He prayed.
- He softened his attitude with sorrow and concern for all involved.
- He determined to act with compassion, regardless.
- He shut his mouth and listened, refusing to be offended.
- He asked rather than broadcasting his agenda.
- He wrapped words that needed to be said in kindness.
- He encouraged each person involved to trust that God desired the best for all.

Wisdom is gained through struggle. We do not like travail but each obstacle overcome is muscle training for our character. Priorities shift. If you have been aimless and drifting, you begin to value commitment. Your focus changes from self-centered to other-centered. The gain of worldly goals shifts to seeking the significant. Trying to do it on your own changes to holding hands with those who care. And, most of all, the feeling that you must figure out your way alone changes to trusting God. The mind's logic joins with the heart's wisdom. You discover the crises of life are gifts that offer you the opportunity to become wiser, more confident, and more caring.

Tragedy Brings Change

Before	After
Aimless and drifting	Committed
Self-centered	Other-centered
Worldly	Dedicated to caring
Life without purpose	Life with clarity and purpose
Life on your own	Life in God's design

Praying to be protected from unexpected problems may be helpful. Praying to overcome them, one step at a time, is more realistic. Even a baby does not welcome his or her birth, but would anyone choose to return to the womb? Ask those who have journeyed through their storm and most would agree that the growth that transpired in difficult times has increased their appreciation for each moment. Happiness is not dependent upon the absence of problems. It is dependent upon confronting problems with grace and without fear. Making big life changes is pretty scary. But know what is even scarier? Regret.

> *Praying to be protected from unexpected problems may be helpful. Praying to be able to overcome them is more realistic.*

Theologian Reinhold Niebuhr wrote a prayer commonly called the Serenity Prayer: "God, grant me the serenity to accept the things I cannot change, to change the things I can, and to have the wisdom to know the difference." Try saying this prayer when you are at a crossroad in the maze of change.

LIFELINES

1. Stacking and flies are part of change.
2. Crisis brings change.
3. Praying to be protected from unexpected problems may be helpful. Praying to be able to overcome them is more realistic.
4. Each of us has the power to make a bad situation worse.
5. It is okay in times of challenge to not have it all figured out.
6. There are many things that are okay in the midst of change.
7. Problems offer two paths: one leads to a more caring and compassionate you; the other leads to a shriveled spirit as you cling to the past.
8. Happiness is not dependent upon the absence of problems but rather confronting them with grace.

The Stories You Believe

You cannot change the past, but you can change
the story that you tell yourself of the past.

■ **ANCHOR: I change the interpretation of my stories by
focusing on the lessons, insights, and strengths I have
gained.**

"I think I am going crazy!" she told me, and she had good reason for such feeling. Her emotions were screaming, begging to
change what could not be changed. Her eight-month-old child
had died from sudden infant death syndrome three months before
our discussion. Those in her support groups—her husband and
the church community—were counseling her to be happy. They
encouraged her to feel blessed that she had birthed a child who
was in heaven and wouldn't suffer like those of us who live life
with its problems!

The young mother was seeking my advice because, though she tried to accept the group's counsel, she could not rid herself of longing for her child. I assured her that her grief was normal and to be expected, even with a deep faith. My hope was to help her appreciate her normal feelings. She was wrong to believe she needed to deny her anguish because of her faith. Healthy faith is with you in your struggle to get up from the ground. It holds you as you slowly stand, encouraging you to move forward. It does not ask that you deny your suffering. Rather, as you move *together*, it whispers hope.

It became clear that there was more to the mother's grief than her articulated concern when she asked, "What do you think happens to aborted babies?" Do you discern her underlying issue? Here was a mother who had an abortion earlier in her life. Perhaps she was too young to care for a child. Maybe she was raped or the child was conceived by incest. Maybe she was wild and loose. Whatever her reason for the abortion, guilt was shaping how she read her story now. How would you have helped her? Your answer will depend upon your beliefs, your understanding of how the three areas of body, mind, and spirit interact, and your own life experiences.

Whether or not you realize it, you are a master storyteller. You tell stories that explain where you've been and where you are going, who you are and who you are becoming. The details of your stories and how you spin them largely determine how you see your life. For instance, if you feel your competence was responsible for a success, you feel able and confident. If you feel the triumph was due to luck, you may dread or shy away from another trial. If others validate your story you feel positive; if they question its validity you either shrink, confused and questioning, or shout the same interpretation repeatedly. The counsel the young mother received by her circle was shaped by the stories *they* believed. Because she could not rid herself of the guilt or overcome her hurt by following their counsel, she sought a way to tell herself a different story.

Be Careful of the Stories You Believe

Stories that help us live life victoriously make us healthy emotionally, physically, and spiritually. They help us understand our experiences. They bring us insight as the biological, psychological, cultural, and spiritual aspects of ourselves adjoin in peace.

Faulty interpretation of our experience is like feeding soap to our emotions and thoughts. The story covers our understanding with a film that dries, leaving a crust. Instead of helping our vision be squeaky clean so light streams insight into our thoughts, we feel unable, as did the young mother. It is in our DNA to seek joy, not just fleeting happiness. That comes when our stories:

> shine light on God's care for each of us,
> affirm our understanding or lead us to a clearer insight,
> illuminate our connectedness to each other,
> assure us from life and its experiences good can come, and
> affirm that each of us has a responsibility to do right, regardless of what others do or say.

Our Story

Our story is influenced by:

> our beliefs
> what we have been taught
> our experiences
> the affirmation of our story by another

Changing the Untruths We Believe

We must interpret our experiences so that our stories help us mature our sense of kindness, humility, grace, and caring. To do so, we must challenge the untruths that attach to difficulties. We can appreciate author Andrea Wachter's books and internet articles that explain how easy it is to develop emotionally unhealthy self-esteem that prohibits us from moving forward in times of hurt. If we have a core sense of shame and inadequacy, and think that a wonderful relationship, body, or job is what makes us valuable, our self-esteem plummets when we experience a loss in that area. The hurt shifts from the actual crisis to criticism of ourselves. We feel unworthy, ugly, stupid, or unable. Nothing external will fix that. These thoughts need an internal upgrade.

For instance, most of us were raised with well-intentioned messages to stop crying immediately (presumably so that we would feel better). Little did our innocent caregivers know that telling us not to cry, or giving us a cookie or a bottle every time we were sad, might give our little brains the message that expressing sadness is not okay and we should find a salve to soothe the emotion. With such messages imbedded from childhood, how are we to handle the flood of emotions that come when we experience significant loss? Feeling we must get past the past and let it go burdens us with tremendous guilt or anger as we struggle with poignant emotions. Self-criticism, depression, and anger imbed. We need to know what is normal when our world falls apart. We need to reject negative messages; instead, we must tell ourselves we are able and we are grateful for the past, for lessons learned, and for the moment.

"I am the screwed-up person you wrote about in *Living Successfully with Screwed-Up People*," a man once said to me. He wasn't asking for advice. He didn't intend to change. So be it!

I liked the man. He had spunk. I hope he liked himself. My lecture that day was on our being pliable, reshaping wrong beliefs, changing, and continuing forward after a misstep. Perhaps he was there to consider the possibility of revising his stories. You can believe stories that make you feel like "nobody likes me" or "I'm not dependable," but instead, why not tell stories that make you feel capable and able?

It isn't easy to be truthful in our stories. We stage our stories to reflect the virtues we admire, the things we believe, or what we have been told. Stories that fill us with doubts, anger, and guilt make regaining balance in our life and relationships much more difficult.

Think about your stories. What do you tell yourself about the people and experiences of your life? What stories do you tell yourself about who you are? The good news for the "screwed-up" man—and for you and me—is that we can restage our stories.

Our well-being depends upon believing stories that are a valid interpretation of our experiences.

Sometimes you don't want to restage your view of a situation because it would force you to be responsible for your part of a problem. Have you visited with family when a night of sharing old memories turned into a fight over politics or faith? Did your words become heated? Did you stew about the situation and the opinionated curmudgeon in the family? Are you now resolved that family get-togethers are not good for anyone?

Restage your story. What did you enjoy about being with your family? Stop any time an idea begins to twist back to your argument. If you are not going to throw someone out of the family, figure out how to handle the situation without being pulled, huffing and puffing, into the fray. Blame games spent on rehashing the past only create hypersensitivity that causes negative flags the next time you are together. Look at the argument with clear vision. Clear vision enables you to recognize your role in the discord and restructure your actions and reactions. This creates a foundation for a next positive experience. If it were science, you would call the family argument a success in many ways. You recognize and value what works and learn what does not work.

The falsehoods we imbed in crisis define us as different, crazy, unworthy, unable, out of control, and stuck. We have amazing power to change these perspectives. Each untruth has two sides: one side tells us that we are unable to overcome our ills while the other side counters that if we adjust our attitude and interpretation of the untruth we can triumph over our woe. Let's look at seven lies that beg to hold us hostage.

Untruth 1: I am different from everyone else.

It is normal to feel isolated, lonely, and cut off when the rug has been pulled out from under you. *The gift*: you recognize that everyone has problems. You are not different or special. But you can be special when you stand back up after a collapse and reach out with care to help others stand.

Untruth 2: I am going crazy.

Your words are jumbled. Your thinking is chaotic. You can't remember. You don't care. You are like a jack-in-the-box with emotions springing in every direction. *The gift*: because your out-of-control emotions come in waves, you are able to survive their attacks and work through their suction, bit by bit.

Untruth 3: I can't.

Torment, affliction, agony, suffering, misery, nightmare, distress, heartache, sorrow, woe, anger—no word seems adequate to describe the vortex of spinning miseries when you have been wronged or lost something precious. *The gift*: you recognize you didn't stand back up on your own. You owe much to supportive friends and family. You know that without God's help the anguish would turn to bitterness.

Untruth 4: I'm unworthy.

Guilt comes packaged in loss or injustice and reigns in low self-esteem. *The gift*: you slowly begin to trust the inner nudging that counters self-inflicted put-downs or the abusive words of others. You begin to recognize strength and/or purpose that flows from surviving the hurt.

Untruth 5: I am naked, exposed, and unable.

Insecurity reigns. To decide, initiate, or act is tiring, almost impossible. It is easier to hide than to expose your unprotected self. *The gift*: you discover others care for you, even with your scars. You discover you are able to do the impossible because you slowly resolve to do so, one step at a time.

Untruth 6: I feel out of control.

Your emotions are askew. Your thinking is defunct. Life feels threatening. *The gift*: you determine to relax and do your best, as you trust that good can come from *anything* and *any situation*.

Untruth 7: I am unable to move forward.

Longing for the treasure of the past is painful. *The gift*: you learn the preciousness of each moment so you have no time to lament what is no more.

You Can Do It!

You can't stop thoughts of your hurts, especially at anniversary times or when you deal with someone or something from your past.

But you can counter feelings that stifle hope and riddle you with self-criticism. You were not born with internal negative statements about yourself or your experiences. You learned to believe you were unable as you met challenges and expectations. If negative is your bent, you can change it without being blasé to reality. Glossing over a wrong with a positive story is harmful and Pollyannaish—recognizing the lesson you have gleaned from the hurt is invaluable. The hurt loses its power to destroy you!

Be real about the situation that brings pain, but refuse to give the hurt power to control your joy. For instance, Kim's death on my birthday could make each year's birthday a slide into longing. Of course I desperately miss her, but I choose to turn my thoughts from *how tragic this day is* to *how grateful I am that I was gifted such a precious child*. It's my birthday and a day I celebrate blessings such as Kim. My children and grandchildren intentionally choose to celebrate Bebe's birthday as opposed to thinking of it as their sister's or mother's death day. No one forgets that Kim died; instead, we are grateful that she lived. Her death awakens our awareness that we should not take our blessings for granted.

Glossing over a wrong with a positive story is harmful and Pollyannaish—recognizing the lesson you have gleaned from the hurt is invaluable.

Sometimes we must simply recognize that our choices or failures were factors in an irreversible crisis. From such times we must choose to learn the lessons and change course. Sometimes we have no control over another's choices that affect us. Let's look at a few more examples of creative triggers (see chapter 5, "Redirecting Your Thoughts and Your Emotions") to overpower negative thoughts from experiences that want to bury you in regret.

- My failed relationship means I am a failure. . . *I am capable of committing and trying to work through relationship failures.*
- If I had been a better parent. . . *I did the best I could for my age and stage.*
- If I had been smarter I would not have failed. . . *I persevered and learned this was not the right course of study for me.*
- If I were thinner or prettier. . . *I am lovable and beautiful in my own way.*
- If I had gotten medical help sooner. . . *I did my best.*
- She hurt my feelings. . . *I am sorry she is losing an opportunity for a friendship.*

Thoughts of sorrow are powerful when I am consumed by anger or hurt from injustice and wrongs. Like prayer, sorrow turns thoughts from self-focus to care for another. The *I-am-sorry-for* thoughts soften my attitude and change my perspective. It is sad when someone destroys a relationship, hurts someone, or does wrong—or equally hurtful when I am responsible for the act. Be assured, those times are remembered when the culprit experiences his or her own difficult period in life. You and I recall failures or wrongs for which we are responsible when we encounter opportunities to repeat the mistake or see someone else doing the same. Life is a teacher.

The Greek philosopher Herodotus said, "Adversity has the effect of drawing out strength and qualities of a man that would have lain dormant in its absence." When you respond positively and constructively to your biggest challenges, the qualities of strength, courage, and character emerge from deep inside of you. Patience, compassion, and an appreciation for the moment grow roots and mature. Difficulties may be the gift that encourages us to counter stories that lock us into believing happiness is hopeless. The entire world is full of suffering. It is also full of overcoming.

Let's be honest. Even when we think we have moved forward we are surprised by sudden overwhelming feelings that throw us into a memory minefield. Why can't we just let go of what can't be changed and move on?

LIFELINES

1. Our emotions are directed by the stories we believe.
2. The healthy way to handle emotions is to recognize, appreciate, and use them.
3. You are in charge of your story, not your emotion.
4. We can redirect our thoughts at any time before, during, or after we find ourselves consumed by loss, injustice, or immoral or wrong actions.
5. Our well-being depends upon believing stories that are a valid interpretation of our experience.
6. Politics is not always about doing the right thing; it is about winning. In life you don't win unless you do what is right.

10

Coping with the Pop-Ups

You can't stop thoughts, but you can refuse to let them play in the attic of your mind.

■ ANCHOR: I am grateful for the warm-fuzzy pop-ups that encourage me, as well as those that vacuum my mind.

We can't forget. Our mind is a computer. Experiences are never deleted. They are stored in files under *pertinent* or *no longer significant*. Pertinent files are relevant memory treasures we want to remember or difficulties we need to resolve. Memories are recalled by intention or are pop-ups that seem to come from the nebulous nowhere. In times of discomfort your intention is to move on and let the past lie, but a thought pulls you back into the fray. Why?

Pop-Up Thoughts

Pop-up thoughts function as part of mental health's two-sided team. The joyful side of the team hangs happy memories on your mental wall, like a *cheerleader.* You know the thoughts—a child brings you a flower, a friend calls you with encouragement, a boss praises your efforts, the sun is shining brightly. These warm fuzzies lighten life as we relish special times together, precious memories of loved ones, and the joys that make life rich. Embrace them.

We can't completely control our thoughts but we do not have to wallow in them.

The janitorial side of the mind's pop-ups is a *vacuum cleaner.* The mind uses it to sweep away the ugly memories that muddle your spirit, the longing, anger, or guilt that keeps you from recognizing the gifts of life. Such pop-ups are uncomfortable, disquieting, and emotionally stressful. They cause your spirit to weaken and heart to harden when the memory is of a friendship broken, harsh words, lost money, destroyed dreams, or failed goals. Even simple memories of an unintentional hurt or wanting something that is denied can be blown into crisis thoughts. You know the feeling. *I can't get my mind off the problem . . . I can't let go . . . I am overwhelmed with the memory . . . I wanted it . . .*

Pop-ups force us to deal with negative life experiences—the losses and hurts—to release their power. These debris-ridding pop-ups are extremely intrusive. They popcorn the very issues that cause us dismay. They may result in an aching throb or be extremely traumatic. For example, if you were molested or abused, such memories are laden with painful emotion. Men and women who have been in combat experience post-traumatic flashbacks. Memories of a difficult relationship may breed fear of entering a new relationship. Such memories harass or disrupt life until the unresolved issues that are toxic to our health and spirit are disclosed and released.

It is hard to stop thinking about a time you were hit below the belt. That cruel thing your teenage daughter said this morning, that worrisome test result the doctor mentioned, the possibility of layoffs at work—banish the thought! The more effort put into avoiding a pesky thought, the faster it pops right back up in your consciousness. It is distressing.

Research shows that when we are actively avoiding an upsetting thought, one part of our brain is busily working to keep it at bay. It is searching out something else to focus on that will protect us from the idea we are trying to avoid. The problem is most thinking is subconscious, so we are able to stop only a tiny fraction of the intrusive thoughts—or even corral them. The reality is that though we cannot completely control our thoughts, we do not have to wallow in them.

Freeing Yourself from the Negative

We are meant to soar as we appreciate the gift of life. Unfortunately, just as the winds can blow a hang glider into rocks, our buried issues can hang us up on the hurt and adversities of life. Some realities are so painful that pretending they are untrue is easier than facing the truth. It is too painful to know your spouse cheats,

The Functions of Pop-Ups

To disclose unclosed or buried issues that are toxic to our health and spirit.

To clean the debris from our thoughts or our mind's storage files—the resentments, anger, and hurts.

To keep painful memories at bay so happy memories can surface.

To teach what works and what does not, what helps and what does not, what to do and what not to do.

To rid us of crippling emotions.

To help us let go of what is no more.

your child is an addict, your parent raped you, or that you are a creep, a liar, or a whatever-is-not-worthy. The list of the things you and I don't really want to know is endless. Freeing a glider from the cliff wall requires strenuous exertion; likewise, freeing yourself from hurt is arduous. It requires we face a painful issue to work through its negative pull. However, when you experience the priceless freedom from a hang-up, you will refuse to allow any impediment to bind you.

Hanging on to longing, anger, and guilt is the debris of life that hardens the heart.

It is very possible that pop-ups are a gift of our spirit to recover the abandon and enthusiasm that adjoins happiness. If something from your past keeps bugging you, do not stuff it into the recesses of your mind. It will keep popping up because it is the mind's job to get rid of the clutter and debris. Let's think together of ways to rid our mind of thoughts that want to pull us back into woe.

Deal with reality.

You will be nagged by the memory until you deal truthfully with your experience. You can't get help for your child who has a problem unless you recognize there is a problem. You can't resolve marriage issues, family discord, a broken friendship, or anything askew unless you confront it with reality. Facing the truth of your experiences is the first step toward mental health and successful living.

A woman described herself as a failure as a mother. Isn't it true that when our children run amok we seek to blame our parenting? Her son was in jail on drug charges. She listed her wrongs: if she had been more encouraging, if she had not pushed him so much in school . . . her beat-me-up list was daunting. Blame games are a waste of time. Regret steals joy and hardens one's spirit. It also puts you in a mode of trying to make up for your wrong, often in unhealthy ways. The truth is, regardless of her parenting skills or lack thereof, her son was the one responsible for his choices, not his mother. Even saints have children who choose a devilish path.

Such trigger phrases as the following lend us courage to let go of the negative and move on:

I am not responsible for what someone else chooses.

I have learned from my mistake.

I am stronger because I overcame.

I appreciate goodness because of that wrong.

I recognize now that choices have long-term consequences.

That is past. I choose to move on.

I'm glad I was strong enough to risk a commitment.

Find ways to be grateful.

Hands down, the most effective way to stop longing for what is no more is to be grateful for the time you shared a relationship, experience, or whatever. I remember driving on a beautiful day, thinking about plans for the weekend, when out of nowhere popped an overwhelming longing for my daughter Kim. Suddenly I was consumed by emotion as the tears flooded and longing filled my being. I

You will be nagged by the pop-ups until you deal truthfully with your experience.

was overwhelmed by thoughts of the times we were together. I longed for her presence. I needed her phone calls, witty remarks, and hugs. I began to pray. *Thank you, God, that it hurts. That means I had a wonderful gift, a relationship that was such a treasure.* This was the switch, the trigger thought, that eased my ache as I said it repeatedly.

Does turning one's spiraling thoughts with a pep talk stop the ache completely? Of course not! Positive thinking won't stop a bee's sting from hurting, but finding the right salve eases the pain. Likewise, finding salve to put on your hurt helps you live with the anguish without bitterness.

A young man whose legs were shot off in Iraq said emphatically, "Do you think 'happy' talk makes the pain go away when I am supposed to walk on these stumps!?" Common sense would respond, "How could it?" His nerves still remind him that a part of his body is gone. Still, he is walking with artificial legs, not giving up when at first he didn't even want to live. I asked him how he turned from depression to acceptance. He replied that initially he saw himself as only half a man, but now when such thoughts pop up, he says, "Thank God I am alive. My friends were not so fortunate." He found a way to see the bigger picture of what he still has rather than centering on what is gone. So must we!

Fair or not, there are wrongs that will never be justifiable to the injured. Sometimes moving on means actively campaigning to stop such injustice from happening again or stepping in to help others injured by the situation. When wrongs cannot be righted, your vision must focus on what you have and can do, as opposed to what is no more. Pop-ups of the hurts will never completely go away. Gratitude is a filter that allows the memory as it pacifies the pain.

Gratitude is a filter that allows the memory as it pacifies the pain.

Being grateful is difficult when the crisis was caused by an unpredictable factor such as a weather-related event. Yet news coverage always finds someone who expresses gratitude for his or her family's survival. How difficult was it for the owners of private oceanfront estates confiscated by the city of Miami, Florida, for development? The city condemned the property for the development of high-rise condominiums to increase the city's tax base.

To the estate owners it felt like theft when the courts approved the condemnation for the common good of the city's residents. The property owners were confronted with the choice each of us struggling with injustice faces: we fill with resentment that swells to acrimony or accept what cannot be changed and move on.

Use the gift of sorrow.

Sorrow is one of the most powerful tools in your arsenal to soften your attitude toward the individual who has done or still does wrong. Repetition of trigger phrases that fill you with sorrow for the culprit keeps stones from filling your heart. Turn your dismay to sorrow for the individual by such phrases as *I am sorry she has such anger. I am sorry they miss the opportunity to be friends. I am so sorry he is missing the opportunity to enjoy his children. I am sorry for all those hurt by this incident.*

It is sad to meet the many who have a cross-off list of people they want to avoid in their family, work, and community. They are surprised that the difficult person seems to pop up everywhere, burning painful memories afresh. These pop-ups continue until we consciously address the issue, acknowledge its hurt, and let it go. Could such times be your spirit encouraging you to choose freedom from the bindings that spin around a screwed-up person or experience?

What if you are the culprit? Being sorry for doing wrong is important, but you must do whatever is necessary to right the wrong; otherwise it will continue to nag you unmercifully.

Lifelines to Free Your Spirit from Pop-Ups

Deal with the reality.
Refuse to allow it any power over your spirit.
Find ways to be grateful.
Use the gift of sorrow.

Irrelevant Except Lessons Learned

You can feel a heavy spirit. It seems as if you are bound, enslaved. Laughter is without lightness. Zest is gone. Be real in such down times; it isn't possible to be up all the time. Still, after you tear up, wipe your eyes and refuse to languish in your angst. It takes courage, tenacity, and determination to choose to change your focus from the sadness or mistakes in life to appreciation of your blessings. Pop-ups are our system's programming to free us from life's debris that wants to hold us in a prison of hurt. If we address the issue, confront it, and refuse to allow it to have power over our happiness, the hurt becomes irrelevant and powerless except as a reminder of the lessons learned. You can houseclean your mind.

No one chooses the music life plays, but each of us chooses how we will dance to it.

The quiet times, the good relationships, and the moments of happiness become richer and more significant after you survive the storm and resolve the issues that keep calling for your attention. The sunrises become more beautiful because you know what it is like in the rain. Has something good begun to peek through your pain—a lesson, a blessing, a new insight, new appreciation? Be encouraged that though you won't be who you were when you began your journey, you are working toward who you will be—a stronger, more grateful, and more caring individual.

LIFELINES

1. Pop-ups can fill you with hope and a sense of joy or be the vacuum cleaners to help you rid your heart of hurt.
2. Controlling your pop-up thoughts is much more difficult when you're under stress, mentally overwhelmed, or just plain exhausted.

3. Hanging on to the longing, anger, and guilt is the debris of life that hardens the heart.

4. Pop-ups force us to deal with negative life experiences to release their power over our emotions.

5. You will be nagged by pop-ups until you deal truthfully with your experiences.

6. The good news is pop-ups lose their pain if you resolve the issue.

7. Healing emotions, like housecleaning, requires clearing out the debris.

8. You won't be who you were before the world fell down around you; you aren't yet who you will be after you journey through the experience.

11

Where Faith and Life Meet

His eye is on the sparrow and I know He watches me.

■ **ANCHOR: I will trust that God has a plan for my life.**

Faith in a God who loves and cares is in crisis when you struggle with catastrophe. Catastrophe isn't the little stuff that we buck up and meet head-on. It is the mind-boggling, can't-fathom-the-next-move, knock-your-feet-out-from-under-you times. In such times the rubber meets the road as we travel through travail either by finding an inner strength as we trust God is with us or by losing hope.

At first, when our emotions are screaming, we may cling to our beliefs. How could we survive this without God? As the pain and chaos loiter we begin to have serious doubts. How could this be God's plan? We question whether such loss, abuse, or injustice could be explained in any way other than horror—certainly not as an opportunity to grow!

We perceive that prayer surely does *not* work, even when multiple people pray; otherwise we wouldn't be suffering from this calamity. We ask, *If God is good, why isn't He good to me? If God is able to do all things, why doesn't He help me?* We wonder, *Why me?*

If deep down you do believe, as we did, you may hope that if you are quiet, you will be out of the bull's-eye in case more disaster is to come. You quietly whisper, "Look somewhere else, Lord. I've handled all I can handle." I imagine you understand. Please don't fear the questions that rise and join hands with doubt.

Questions are a sure sign your faith is being forged, changing from iron to steel. In the midst of crying, "Why have You deserted me?" you will discover a deepening understanding of who God is and His purpose for your life.

Mother Teresa wrote to her superiors seeking counsel for her despair and doubts after working with the multitude suffering poverty and pain on a daily basis. Her efforts seemed insignificant. According to the World Bank, at that time 90 percent of the population in India was below the poverty line. Desperate parents sold their children to pimps, their babies to strangers, and their body's organs to survive. Mother Teresa was in a flood of need. She asked, "Why, God, would You not stop the abysses swallowing your children?"

In one of her letters she wrote, "Where is my faith? Even deep down . . . there is nothing but emptiness and darkness. . . . If there be God—please forgive me. When I try to raise my thoughts to Heaven, there is such convicting emptiness that those very thoughts have no faith. Repulsed, empty, no faith, no love, no zeal. . . . What do I labor for?"[1] Thankfully, we know from Mother Teresa's continued service and testimonies that she worked through her doubts and in their place was a solid belief and trust in God her Father.

A life without trial may not struggle with faith. For those of us who do, the very struggle births a deeper realization that life without God is empty and hope is withered. If at this moment you are feeling little hope, listen to God's whispers. Be encouraged that in the midst of aloneness filled with riveting questions, faith is forged. A sure knowledge of God's care is birthed. Faith that has gone through the fire sharpens our hearing of God's still, small voice. Ancient wisdom affirms an inverted logic: *in our weakness we are made strong; in dying we are born to a richer life.* Great doubts, deep wisdom . . . small doubts, little wisdom.

Great doubts, deep wisdom . . . small doubts, little wisdom.

Finding God in the Questions

We are often surprised by unexpected experiences that confirm there is something beyond our understanding guiding—maybe even protecting—us. Some of these experiences are daunting. They don't fit our understanding. We are bewildered and hide the experience from others for fear of being perceived as fanatical or crazy.

I had such an experience in Italy. My husband, Paul, was in the United States seeking employment opportunities. I took our two children for our last jaunt in Europe to enjoy a certain beach before my husband's military commitment in Germany ended. The sky-blue ocean was twenty feet from our cottage door. It was the wonderful, just-be-together fun that I imagine many of you enjoy at the beach with your family or friends! The children played in the cold water and gritty sand and then ran inside the cottage to shower under warm water.

Our five-year-old son Paul went inside to shower while I watched Kim. When his stay seemed long, I checked and found him singing in the shower. I returned to the beach chair and began work on a needlepoint. Within moments, some invisible force literally shook my shoulder and commanded, *Get Paul!* I ran to the cottage to find Paul on the floor of the shower, unconscious and not breathing.

It seemed an eternity before I could see any signs of respiration, and then Paul's breathing was erratic. His near death was from carbon monoxide poisoning caused by the antiquated water heating system. Gas shot through an open pipe under the water tank to heat the shower's water. When the bathroom door was shut, the flame burned up the oxygen, expired, and the gas shot directly into the air. The room filled with gas mixed with carbon monoxide, a poisonous combination.

I can explain the cause of Paul's near tragedy, but there is no logical explanation of the command that shook me into frantic action. I just know Paul is here without any repercussions because he is supposed to be. That doesn't explain why two children visiting Italy from Switzerland the previous summer were brain-damaged in such a shower. Such mysteries defy logic that even the pious have diligently tried to answer through theological debate, the "Why do bad things happen to good people?" question.

It should be obvious from my life experience that things do not always work out the way we hope, regardless of prayer or belief. Still, there are moments in our life for which there seems no rational explanation yet we know they are real. We have a sure knowledge that there is something outside the bounds of our understanding. Such experience keeps faith breathing when the pangs of pain seem to have no end and doubts threaten to extinguish the flame.

Holding It Together

We grow up believing, or come to belief by reasoning, that faith is the best understanding of life. But in times of travail, we wonder, *Is what I believe real? Is there purpose in this life?* We want to know that good can come from such hurt. How could it be so in such trauma? I didn't question *why* my child died. She had a virus. It was my holding-it-together that caused the questions.

My "doing" came to a halt on an Emmaus Walk retreat, an excellent time of study and reflection. I went, prodded by friends who thought it would be helpful. I wondered if I really wanted to learn more about God. Please don't be shocked by my honesty. It is tough to be pious when your child is in a casket in the ground. I imagine some of you who are struggling through your own loss understand.

> When life is askew, questions are the fertilizer of a growing and deepening faith.

On the retreat, a professional at my table spent endless time lamenting her busy life. She didn't have time to fulfill her responsibilities at work or at home. Who does? It seemed so petty. Surely she had the intelligence to *figure it out!* It was as if a weight overwhelmed my soul. I fled to be alone and to scream to God. *It isn't fair! We didn't complain when caring for Lee, whose diabetes caused her to be so fragile. We helped her grow into a charming, outgoing, happy child with a health problem, not a handicap. Wasn't that enough? When LeeAnne died we kept going and trusting. So why haven't You taken this pain away? Are You there? If so, don't You care?*

I screamed internally, uncovering what I had masked. As I wept so hard my spirit filled with peace—as unexpectedly as my need to flee from the retreat center. I surrendered. I couldn't change what was, nor did I have enough strength to survive our loss, even with the help of family and friends. My faith became simple: *I can live without LeeAnne and I can live without health, wealth, or anything else, but I can't live with the emptiness and hopelessness I feel when I wall God out. I simply know God is because without Him there is no hope.*

Solid Faith

Suffering and trouble send us into seven normal and healthy stages toward recovery, each replete with questions:

1. Shock. *I can't believe this has happened to me!*
2. Sorrowful questioning. *God, why did You let this happen?*
3. Anger. *God, this isn't right!*
4. Fear. *Lord, will it get worse?*
5. Despair (many get bogged down here). *I will never recover!*
6. Searching. *Lord, what lesson or benefit do You have for me through this suffering?*
7. Accepting. *Yes, Lord, I trust!*[2]

It is not possible to come out of the deep darkness of a catastrophe whole and without bitterness if your faith is unhealthy. Faith that is pie-in-the-sky and knows all the answers doesn't work in the down and dirty times of life. Pious clichés and easy answers only add fuel to the dismay. Times of struggle demand a hard-core faith that allows you to question, stomp, and cry out. It is crying out, beating the ground, begging, reasoning, and saying what you feel and what you need that frees you to reach up to walk hand in hand with God. A spirit able to soar out of the pit of agony requires faith that helps you look up when everything in you cries for you to give up.

> *You need a hardcore faith that allows you to question, stomp, and cry.*

Life is seldom quiet long. When our daughter Kim was battling leukemia and its multiple health issues, we were back in the lions' den. Kim so wanted to live, and though she knocked at death's door several times, miraculously her leukemia appeared to be in remission after her three-year struggle. Little did we know she was on death's precipice as we celebrated Christmas and her remission. Two months later she died, leaving a husband, four precious children, and broken hearts throughout our community.

The day before she died, her aunt Amy felt compelled to visit Kim while the rest of the family was at work and school. Kim shared memories of the special times with her husband and children and the support of dear family and friends. As her time on this side of life was drawing to an end, they talked of feeling God's presence and His angelic beings. How grateful we are that Amy was there, laughing and remembering with Kim. God was filling Kim's spirit with peace. Amy wrote of her experience that day with Kim to share with our family. You will find that letter in the appendices. Perhaps reading it will be an incentive for you to reach out when you feel urged to call, visit, or offer support to someone who suddenly begins to command your mind's attention.

Do you recall such an experience, a time you felt drawn to do or say something that proved to make a difference, a time someone called you in a moment of need, an answer to a problem that jumped out of your reading, or a dream that provided an answer to a dilemma? It is as if your spirit is working behind the scenes and a realm unseen is interplaying with your life. Journal such times, for seeing those recollections in print will encourage you to be aware of the small coincidences or whispers that seem to affirm you are not alone. We will talk more about this mystery in the next chapter.

Trusting God is a choice that is incredibly freeing.

Throughout time, people have recognized that we operate on two levels: the rational that can be seen and measured and the sphere beyond human comprehension that belongs in the realm of the gods. Unhealthy religion emphasizes a separation from the chaos and confusion of life. It strives to make life simple and offers dogma and clichés for withdrawal from life's problems. But in real

Key Understandings of Faith

Grief is a God-given response to hurts, losses, and
wrongs, not a sign of lack of faith.
Trusting God includes telling Him what you really feel,
not what you think you ought to feel.
It is all right and healthy to ask questions about your
faith. Being honest with God frees you to walk with
Him as opposed to trying to hold it together on your
own.

life, in the day-to-day responsibilities, we are suspended between
the extremes of order and confusion, the known and unknown,
the duties and wants. Only when we trust God's care are we able to
live comfortably in this tension. I use the word *comfortably* loosely
here, for loss and wrongs always put us on a journey through hard
places. It is that very process that deepens faith, even if at first we
struggle and reject the idea of a caring God.

Faith does not imply simply accepting the hurts of life as if we
have no voice; instead we must share our anguish, plead our case,
and then walk our path, trusting that from even such as this good
can come. I hope our faith becomes like that of Christ. Fearing His
death, He pled to God. He was in such anguish that He sweated
blood and railed at His disciples. But after He expressed His concerns and prayed His desires, He was filled with peace and resolve
to walk the rest of His journey with quiet acceptance. Addressing
our issues and concerns frees us to deal with reality. Faith is like
the hope that lights a candle in even the darkest situation. We can
say with acceptance, "It is what it is. Thank You, Lord."

Perhaps the thought that God cares seems like fanatically clinging to nonreality. Yet inside you feel Him and hear His voice, so
why not trust Him? Could it be that troubles are our training

ground? Troubles reset priorities, grow empathy, and forge faith into simplicity. How difficult it is to see such travail as a gift. But perhaps it is. Unwanted . . . daunting . . . life-changing!

LIFELINES

1. Great doubts, deep wisdom . . . small doubts, little wisdom.
2. Faith needs to be hardcore to allow you to question, stomp, and cry.
3. Plugging along isn't enough.
4. When life is askew, questions are the fertilizer of a growing and deepening faith.
5. A spirit that soars out of the pits of agony requires faith that helps you look up when everything in you cries for you to give up.
6. Hanging on to what cannot change devastates life.
7. Trusting God is a choice that is incredibly freeing.

12

The Help
beyond Understanding

My religion consists of a humble admiration of the illimitable superior spirit who reveals himself in the slight details we are able to perceive with our frail and feeble mind.

Albert Einstein

■ ANCHOR: I listen to the voice speaking within my spirit.

When in crisis it is difficult to think that such an injustice, wrong, or tragedy is in the "plan" for our life. Yet quite commonly in the midst of such times we experience such inexplicable happenings that we ponder whether there is a design to life beyond our understanding. Stories abound of surviving the nonsurvivable, comprehending the incomprehensible, and seeing the impossible become possible. We question. Are these things happenstance? Luck? Coincidence? Chance?

Our daughter Kim was sick enough to consider hospitalization the night before her death, but after so many hospitalizations she wanted to attempt to recuperate at home. Kim's husband called the following morning to ask that I check on her in the early afternoon.

I went to the grocery store to pick up some soup and goodies she would need after she awakened. As I was shopping, I was suddenly overcome by a need to go immediately to Kim's. I left and sped toward her home. As I turned onto her street, still a mile from her home, an ambulance with siren blaring was turning into her driveway. Coldness filled my soul. I knew. Kim had died.

Unexplainable moments of sure knowledge happen throughout life. Years before, my husband had awakened in the wee hours of the morning with a compelling need to take LeeAnne to the hospital. Paul wanted verification that her flu-like symptoms were innocuous. The medical team examined LeeAnne. She talked about her puppies and baby brother. All the physicians agreed with Paul's diagnosis of flu. Then, as Paul lifted her to the bed, her eyes dilated. She died in her father's arms.

At this same time that Paul was with the physicians trying to save LeeAnne's life, my father was being wheeled from the same medical center after being hospitalized for three months, held to life by a respirator in critical care with myriad complicating problems: enterovirus, a polio-like virus no adult had survived; pseudomonas, a bacterial infection that kills the young and strong; and multiple myeloma cancer. His medical team's prognosis was sure death. His remarkable survival has been published in *JAMA*, a medical journal. How could such timing be mere coincidence—my healthy daughter arrives to die as her dying grandfather leaves to live more years?

After LeeAnne's death I reflected on what seemed to be more than chance. It was a blessing Paul awoke and was compelled to take LeeAnne to the hospital for consultation. For Paul, a physician, it was comforting to know other physicians saw no evident signs of the encephalitis that destroyed her brain. He had not missed some sign others could see.

Other things may seem inconsequential: the week before six-year-old LeeAnne's death from viral encephalitis, I purchased a suit for my growing twelve-year-old son, ordered two hundred personalized note cards, and had a photo session of LeeAnne—minutia I had procrastinated doing for months. Certainly these were not mind-boggling coincidences or predictors of the crisis, but each lessened the stress as we dealt with planning the ceremony and writing notes to caregivers. Who is thinking of clothes or stationery when burying a child? I was grateful we had those last photos of LeeAnne. Merely chance? Perhaps.

Those of faith believe this sense within to be God's Holy Spirit, opening us to a sure knowledge, an uncanny awareness separate from our logic and understanding. Such experiences seem to affirm that there is more to life than we scientifically understand. It is especially in difficult times that it seems a spirit within whispers hope and encourages us to make steps toward recovery. Sometimes the sense seems to be a command to action, as I felt when my six-year-old son was gassed in a beach house shower in Italy. But most often this sense is a mere urge or nagging nudge to do something.

A woman shared her pesky reoccurring thought to call an acquaintance with whom she had no contact since college. It seemed ludicrous to think the friend's old telephone number would be current. But she called and, sure enough, her friend from the past answered. After an hour-long conversation, this long-forgotten acquaintance confided, "I had a gun in my hand when the phone rang. I felt compelled to answer. You saved my life."

Sometimes the urge seems irrelevant to the dramatic occurrence that it births. A patient of my husband was at the end stage of kidney failure. His wife wanted to help him with his bucket list dream of going to the Indianapolis 500 race before his inevitable demise. The grueling effort required was a logistical nightmare with his medical paraphernalia, but the couple managed. On the return flight home, the wife shared this venture with a flight attendant. The attendant replied, "I've always wanted to be an organ donor. I could give a kidney." The flight attendant was serious, and to everyone's amazement he was a perfect match. You can feel confident that the couple, as well as the attendant, sensed there was more to the experience than sheer luck.

A man described his tension with a sister whose advice and correction came with his every move after his wife's death. Her admonitions were driving him crazy. He planned to cut her from his life. As he started to ask her to leave, a sense of peace and caring overwhelmed him. Instead of reaming her with criticism, he put his hand on her shoulder, thanking her for loving and supporting his wife and family. "It was uncanny. It was so not 'me' speaking and feeling love for her. It had to be God."

Sometimes dreams convey a plan. Perhaps our brain simply works through problems as we sleep or our thoughts are stirred by something beyond explanation. R. J. LeTourneau was an ironmonger and welder with no professional education. He owned a contracting business to move dirt for such projects as the road to the Hoover Dam in Nevada. One night he awoke with a detailed plan for the construction of earthmoving equipment and engineering vehicles. The plan was decades ahead of its time, using low-pressure rubber tires and electric wheel drive in earthmoving. He trusted his vision as God's guidance. Building on that vision, he became recognized worldwide for the development and manufacture of heavy engineering vehicles. Seventy percent of the vehicles used by the Allies in WWII were designed by LeTourneau. He licensed hundreds of patents and built five manufacturing plants worldwide for his earthmoving equipment. He attributed all of his plans to an inner sense within that seemed to guide his vision.

Tina Thomas, a nurse specializing in children's care, shared that multiple times in her career, as she walked down the hospital corridor, she felt an overwhelming and compelling urge, almost a push, to enter a child's room. Each time she found the child in distress, too near death to call for help. Had she not been there at that moment, the child would have died.

Sandy Cox shared feeling sudden, extreme thirst as she sat reading her book on the patio. She went inside but remembered the glass she had left by the patio chair. She turned to retrieve it but was stunned to see a ball of lightning rolling down the hill of her backyard. It exploded on her lawn chair. She stated, "I would have been electrocuted if I had been sitting in the chair."

Such tales of the unexplainable are mysteries that defy our scientific understanding and beg for explanation. Few feel comfortable declaring themselves blessed or protected when others are not. We struggle with questions that ask why bad things happen to good people. That squeamish feeling of doubt was evident in an interview with a heroic fireman after the Twin Towers catastrophe on 9/11. The fireman shared for twenty minutes multiple near-death episodes as he helped a group descend the stairs from the sixtieth floor. The dark stairwell was filled with smoke and fallen debris. Explosions hurtled missiles of plaster and steel as they descended. Fire exploded into the stairwell from hallways moments after the group passed. Within minutes of the group's escape into the promenade, the stairs collapsed, leaving a gaping hole in the building's side. The fireman concluded his interview: "We were so lucky!" Listeners were

Looking back is often when we feel there has been a scientifically unexplainable guide helping us.

stunned that anyone could have survived the escape. How could it have been luck? Yet many did not escape. We are left with the unexplainable.

A television evangelist interviewed parents whose child's recovery appeared miraculous. His words implied that it was prayer and their faith that saved the child. I certainly would not question the power of prayer and faith. However, it would have been tragic if we questioned whether our child's death was the result of our ineffective prayers or lack of faith. We didn't play with such thoughts. Bad things happen to good people, faith-filled people, who do not doubt the possibility of a miracle. Miracles happen to agnostics and atheists without prayer. We, figuratively, see through eyes that are dim. We do not understand many of the mysteries.

I believe as you journey through loss and hurt you will hear and feel a voice within you. It may be earthshaking counsel or simply a nudge. Perhaps you have experienced a sure knowledge, dreamed of a future event, or felt a sudden urge to reach out. Maybe someone called you or did something just at a moment you needed his or her care. Have you felt a sudden anxiety urging you not to do something you were planning? Don't brush off the nudges. As you trust your inner sense, you will begin to feel clear indications that you are not "alone" in this life.

Personal Experience

I don't know where you are in your experience, but I do know that in the tough times I wanted an umbrella over my head to keep the bad away. Maybe I wouldn't be in the line of fire if I just stayed quiet and out of sight. I was hiding from the rain when, three months after our daughter Kim died, my editor at Revell, Lonnie Hull DuPont, emailed. She asked if I wanted to write another book and suggested the topic that became the title of this book: *Standing Up When Life Falls Down Around You.*

I stumbled around the idea, for that was where I was: trying to stand. Certainly I needed to focus on the keys to surviving and thriving. As I struggled with the incumbent issues of the death of our second daughter, I began to write. I weighed how to handle the problems with grace, what helped, and what did not. Lonnie's outreach was a gift that focused me on sharing the real process of getting up and going on rather than simply reiterating clichés that belittle the effort. I am deeply grateful. Was her call merely coincidence? I don't believe so.

Begin journaling the "coincidences" that turn you from a mistake, prevent a problem, or simply encourage your moment. Record the times you feel strangely compelled to call someone or offer support. Remember the times something unexpected changed your day for the better. Jot down the unanticipated support that came just at the moment you were overcome with hopelessness. Write the verse or story line that seemed to jump out as you read. Recall experiences that were uncanny and simply unexplainable. It appears our internal guidance system is actively steering us toward recovery and joy.

I have a little plaque in my kitchen window that reads, "Because someone we love is in heaven, a little bit of heaven is in our home." That may be wishful thinking, but the longer I live and the more I see and learn, the more I recognize there is more to this life than just what is visible or scientifically understandable. For certain I know that the more I trust the voice within me, the fewer times I stumble as I handle life's ups and downs. Also, the more I stop to consider the coincidences that come at the needed moment, the more I feel upheld. Looking back is often when I note that something unexplainable has guided my path. It seems to me that when life is the most challenging is when we find deeper powers within. What does your experience tell you?

LIFELINES

1. Discoveries are heightening the awareness of how interconnected even the simplest particles of life are, and how these connections influence us, even when separated by space, time, or differences.

2. Looking back is often when we note something unexplainable has been our guide.

3. Your internal guidance system is actively steering you toward joy.

4. When life is the most challenging is when we find deeper powers within.

Letting It Go

When you forgive, you in no way change the past—
but you do change the future.

■ **ANCHOR: I refuse to allow a wrong to imprison me.**

Elizabeth Smart, the fourteen-year-old daughter of a close-knit
Mormon family, was kidnapped from her home in the middle
of the night by a religious fanatic, Brian David Mitchell, and his
wife, Wanda Barzee. Elizabeth was chained, dressed in disguise,
repeatedly raped, and told she and her family would be killed
if she tried to escape. She was rescued on March 12, 2003, and
rejoined her family to pick up the pieces of her life after nine
months in captivity. She would have been justified in pinpointing
her nightmarish experience as the crucible for a ruined life. How
was she to forgive the torture she endured? Elizabeth's mother
had advice.

Elizabeth, this is important. Listen to me. What this man has done is terrible. There aren't any words that are strong enough to describe how wicked and evil he is. He has taken nine months of your life that you will never get back again. But the best punishment you could ever give him is to be happy and move forward with your life. To do exactly what you want. . . . If you hold on to your pain or dwell on what has happened, that is allowing him to steal more of your life away. You keep every second for yourself. . . . God will take care of the rest.[1]

Elizabeth determined to take back her life. She testified in the criminal case against Mitchell and Barzee, seeking justice without fear or thoughts of revenge, for she trusted that no matter the outcome, God would be the ultimate judge. She became proactive, using her experience to create a foundation to help prevent crimes against children. In 2012 her fairy-tale wedding to Matthew Gilmour, a young man she met while on a church mission in Paris, made the cover of *People* magazine. She refused to give more of her life to the people who had so mistreated her. You, too, can refuse to give any more of your life to a misfortune.

Forgiving is a personal choice that changes you inside out.

What Is Forgiveness?

Too often we think forgiving someone is about the other guy. Forgiveness is about freedom for the one who forgives. According to author Suzanne Woods Fisher, most Protestant traditions assert that forgiveness begins with God, that we receive it and *then* are able to forgive others. However, the Amish believe they receive forgiveness from God *only* if they extend forgiveness to others, because God forgives only the penitent.[2] That may help you understand why within hours of the shooting and killing of five girls in an

Amish school in Pennsylvania in 2006, the parents of the children responded with forgiveness to the shooter's wife and family.

The problem is not *the act of forgiving*, which was primary in their beliefs; it is *healing* from the hurt. The act of letting go of hurts is counterintuitive to our nature. Yet it is essential to our well-being. Elizabeth Smart forgave her kidnappers and the Amish forgave the shooter; even the most grievous horrors can be let go. It is the healing that takes time and effort, even after the words "I forgive" are voiced. Healing must process life in and out so joy can return. It takes *time* and resolute *determination*.

How will you know you have forgiven?

- Your mind does not fill with anger when the memory of the hurt pops up.
- You no longer hide from or try to avoid the culprit.
- You feel compassion when he or she is in your mind or presence.

Understanding the Act of Forgiving

Let's consider a key understanding of the act of forgiving: *forgiveness is the act that frees the person who forgives.*

Forgiving isn't just a theological term. Forgiving is an action that frees the person who forgives from allowing the slight, injustice, or loss to reign in his or her heart. It is a personal decision that changes you inside out, the key to unlock yourself from hurts inflicted by others or by self. To not forgive is like drinking poison in the hopes that the other person will die. Clinging to the wrong of your failure or wound is not penance; it is self-flagellation.

Wrongs need to be *recognized*, *grieved*, and *forgiven*. Hiding hurt or running from its memory locks it behind closed doors. Unreleased, the hurt seeps toxins into our life. So why do we find it so difficult to let go of issues and release ourselves from anguish? It is because hanging on to the negatives in life does have heavy-duty bonuses.

- Lessons are *learned*: once stung, I will not be stung again.
- Bragging rights are *earned*: I have endured more than you.
- Being a victim is *justified*: if I quit crying it will minimize my injury.

I imagine you know several people who are hardened and caustic after dealing with their crisis's seeping toxins. Bitterness pours forth negatives into their thoughts, words, reactions, and focus. Their attitude becomes *nothing is right; everything has a catch; no act is selfless.* "She has never been the same since . . ." is a tragic excuse to give up celebrating life.

If you are having a difficult time moving forward, be aware that you probably believe that:

- Letting go would imply you have forgotten. *How could I?*
- Letting go lets the culprit off the hook. *Why should I?*
- Letting go feels impossible. *How can I?*
- Letting go is too difficult. *Why can't I handle this?*

Forgiveness Must Be Unconditional

To let go of the hurts that want to bind our joy, we must recognize that our forgiveness must be unconditional.

A mother in Fresno, California, stood in the question-and-answer portion of a seminar I was concluding on death and dying. "Could you help me?" she asked. "I know I need to forgive the teenager who was babysitting my three-year-old son. She was talking to her friends on her cell phone when Mickey fell into the pool. Mickey's death was an accident, but I can't forgive her if she doesn't apologize. Her excuses tell me she just doesn't recognize that her irresponsibility cost a life."

I agreed that this mother was owed an apology. The problem is that a precondition turns *forgiveness* into *negotiation*. If the culprit fails to meet the prerequisite, you must stuff or hide your hurt behind a closed door within your mind. Would an apology help this grieving mother? I believe so, but imagine how you would feel if someone who owes you an apology for an egregious tragedy—or even for the simplest hurt—acknowledges and apologizes for his or her culpability. Wouldn't you need more than "I'm sorry" to assuage your pain?

Forgiveness is not about the other guy. It is about your choice to not allow the wrong to steal any more of your happiness. Freedom from a hurt demands you forgive as God forgives—freely. No stipulations allowed. Verbal forgiving as opposed to heart forgiving puts you on alert, watching for more signs of culpability. You know the idiom—hurt me once, shame on you; hurt me twice, shame on me!

> *Forgiveness is an act; healing is a journey.*

The Bible is chock-full of rifts in relationships—brother against brother, wife against husband, child against parent, nation against nation. Recently a young woman left the medical world to work in a nonprofit organization. She stated how she looked forward to working with people in supportive relationships. She wanted no more politics and nit-picking. Unfortunately, she found such difficulties existed even in a faith-based organization. Regardless of whether the relationship is within a business, family, friend, church, or world context, people see their experiences through different lenses. Differences in perspective are the politics of life that require negotiation, compromise, and ultimately forgiveness.

You may be hung up on the feeling that if you forgive an offender you will be letting him or her off the hook. But the reality is no one is able to "unhook" someone else. The wrongdoer is responsible for his or her acts and their consequences, forgiven or not. If you are going to heal, you've got to feel the pain, express your anguish, and let go of the hurt. Suppressed feelings cause abscesses of the soul.

It is holy work that files painful hurts under "irrelevant, except for lessons learned."

Forgiving requires holy work, work of the spirit within each of us to file the memory under "irrelevant, except for lessons learned." *Recognizing your need* for forgiveness is humbling. *Accepting it* is freeing. *Giving it* cuts the bonds that tie you to injuries, slights, and wrongs. *Learning from it* is a gift.

How Do I Forgive?

Discern the truth.

Do not excuse away or justify wrong. Elizabeth Smart needed affirmation that the man who kidnapped her was a villain. Draping him in excuses for his wrong would pervert right thinking.

Be real about your situation.

You can be content in the most difficult relationship, with limits and boundaries, as long as you do not spin off someone else's behavior. If you stay in reactive mode, you slowly warp as sarcasm and bitterness walk with you during the day and sleep with you at night. The unforgiven wrong gnaws through the façade of reconciliation. Without mercy, the relationship splinters and walls build.

Pray for the wrongdoer.

Prayer *slowly* fills you with grace—grace to forgive and to be kind and caring. Prayer fills you with a sure sense that you are not handling your problem alone and opens you to whispers from your spirit. Know you are not the only one who cares about the person who does wrong.

Soften critical remarks that tie you to the injustice.

Adjust your self-talk to sadness for the scoundrel or negative situation. Stones fill your heart when the focus is the unfairness, hurt, or wrong. The more stones you carry, the darker your life becomes as heaviness washes over your spirit. Be tenacious to keep your angry thoughts at bay while interjecting kinder ones.

Elizabeth Smart's captor believed he had the right to kidnap and rape her. He did not apologize. Nor did the shooter of the Amish children apologize. Both Elizabeth and the Amish forgave for *their own* benefit. Neither wanted to be imprisoned by the person who had stolen an irretrievable part of their life. They chose to forgive because they believed forgiveness is God's key to letting go of a hurt that can enslave the one wronged. In many ways, someone's intentionally hurting you gifts you with insight and gratitude for those who have integrity.

See life for what it is—your life *imprisoned* by anger and anguish over the past or *freed* by a forgiving spirit. You are not responsible for the attitudes and responses of other people in your life, but you are responsible for *you*. Do it right, regardless of what someone else does. Is that difficult? Of course! Pain may be the fist that knocked you down, but forgiveness is the hand that will help you stand.

LIFELINES

1. A bad start, sad years, or hard times should not be the end of your world.
2. Forgiving with strings attached binds your freedom to someone else's willingness to comply.

3. It is holy work that files painful hurts under "irrelevant, except for lessons learned."

4. Differences are the politics of life that require negotiation, compromise, and ultimately forgiveness.

5. *Recognizing your need* for forgiveness is humbling. *Accepting it* is freeing. *Giving it* cuts the bonds that tie you to injuries, slights, and wrongs. *Learning from it* is a gift you give yourself.

6. Suppressed feelings cause abscesses of the soul.

7. Refusing to be captive to injustice and hurts is the choice that changes you inside out.

8. Turning a thought to mercy softens the spirit instead of hardening the heart.

9. Pain may be the fist that knocked you down, but forgiveness is the hand that will help you stand.

Dealing with Family and Friends

The shortest distance between two points is the route you travel in the company of a friend.

■ ANCHOR: I will let those who care know *what helps* and *what does not help*.

It is rare to want to be with friends when your world has fallen down around you. Withdrawal from usual social interactions is normal. Interacting with others is tedious. You feel isolated, disinterested, and alone, even in a crowd. With friends and family, you feel marked.

Relax. You don't have to rush to be with others after being struck by lightning. They won't forget you, and healing requires alone time. Look at our animal friends. When they are injured, they burrow into a corner, away from activity, to lick their wounds. It's okay to be self-absorbed for a while. If, however, your isolation period lengthens and pushes you further and further from relationships and socialization, your health may be at risk.

We all need hugs. The heart weakens and the spirit withers if you stay in your cave. Being involved with and feeling part of a circle of family and friends is critical for health, especially in difficult times. It turns out social isolation is actually one of the biggest risk factors for human mortality. The risk to our well-being by low social interaction is

as dangerous as being an alcoholic,

as harmful as never exercising,

twice as dangerous as obesity, and

incites an inflammatory factor implicated in leukemia, cardiovascular disease, and autoimmune disorders such as Alzheimer's disease, osteoporosis, rheumatoid arthritis, and some forms of cancer.[1]

The problem is we have unreal expectations of family and friends when we travel through life's valleys. It is okay and right to expect those who care for us to gather around when we go through hard times. We need their understanding, empathy, and encouragement. We trust they know us well enough to excuse our behavior as we cry and harangue. However, too often they have limited patience and offer coping advice that feels judgmental. Even those who do attend us well during such times frequently pull away before we are ready to climb from their arms. As our anguish continues we may blame our caregivers for not offering support that lessens our sorrow. Such is not fair, but it is the way it is. Equally unfair is that when we are hurting we often target those in our safety zone, the very ones who are our support. Ask any parent of a troubled teenager who receives a hard time.

My husband attended a patient in the hospital whose room was filled with cards and flowers. He commented that she must have many friends. She held up a notepad and said, "You can bet I'm keeping a list of those who don't do something! They won't expect anything from me!" She had a tough measuring stick. *Appreciating* those who reach out with care, whatever it is and for whatever period of time it is, rather than *expecting* makes life much sweeter.

Some of us are fortunate that those dear to us are by our side the whole journey. They are the rare birds. It is more likely that support is intensive at the beginning of your devastation and then family and close friends cry out for the "old you." That may feel pushy as they try to help you get back on track. It may seem to be desertion when they give you space to resolve your issues. Perhaps those on the periphery cause you to feel diseased as they flee from your presence muttering a cliché such as "Life goes on!"

Innocent comments or acts can sting, even when there is no such intention. One friend commented to a recent divorcée, "Great news! Now you are back in the market. Lucky you!" Another man said he didn't have a phone call or visit from his parents for more than a month after his son's funeral. His parents lived a mile away. A son shared that his mother blamed him for his cancer because he ate unwashed fruit with its poisons. A couple whose baby died from SIDS wept as they recalled their shock. They returned home after taking their baby to the hospital morgue to find every baby item in their home gone. Their caring and concerned parents feared such items would add to their distress, so they removed them all from the home. The emptiness added to the devastation.

No doubt you have been stunned by an insensitive remark. A man shared with horror his own open-mouth-and-insert-foot comment. His friend's son, wife, and two grandchildren were killed in a car accident. It was the impetus for him to increase his own life insurance. Leaving his insurance agent's office, he encountered the friend whose tragedy had spurred his action. Without thinking, he blurted out, "I was shocked by the horrible accident. My word, I imagine the insurance company will have to pay out big for that tragedy!"

The comment was a major faux pas and could be a permanent scar in the grief-stricken father's memory, even if he recognized his friend's mortification after such a gaffe. The only way to put salve on the hurt from such an inappropriate remark was for the embarrassed man to apologize to his grieving friend and explain why insurance was foremost in his thoughts. Ask anyone who has walked through the fire of catastrophe and they will popcorn such tactless remarks or acts that have burned into their memory.

It may help you forgive a friend's insensitive comment if you consider that the friend is also stunned by your devastation. He or she is unsure of what is best to say or do and wants to be there for you in your difficult time. Without a doubt, your friend would also wonder how he or she could possibly handle such a tragedy. Surely, the friend who holds your hand and says the wrong thing is made of dearer stuff than the one who shies away.

The friend who holds your hand and says the wrong thing is made of dearer stuff than the one who shies away.

We are partially to blame if those from whom we need support do not read our unexpressed needs. Though you are typically brave and not used to asking for help, be aware that when you tell your friends and family you do not need help, they will think it seems disrespectful to insist. We need to ditch the belief that there is any value in being the strong and silent man or woman. Being silent isn't being strong; it is being a victim.

Hopefully we express our needs and grievances more graciously than my husband's patient, who was ready to scratch off the culprits from her list of friends! It is foolish to hold tightly the false belief that we can handle problems on our own strength. Such bravado is no wiser than trying to cross a set of monkey bars without letting go of the bar we hold. We are left hanging, not moving forward.

Sometimes, even if you let your needs be known, an individual does not reach out as you hope. A woman listed a litany of valid reasons she was hurt by and furious at her children for their lack of support as she battled cancer. But she needed to shake off the hurt; it only intensified her pain and did nothing to change the reality.

Being silent isn't being strong; it is being a victim.

It helps to understand that until we go through a devastating experience, most of us are blind to the crucial support needed. I suggested to her, "Your children love you. They have no experience with such a difficulty. They see you as the parent who always solves the problems. They believe your health crisis is merely a hurdle." Thinking more kindly toward those whose behavior stings soothes the emotional pain.

No one can make another person empathetic, but each of us is responsible for sharing our needs when we travel through life's valleys. There is no guarantee, even when you express your needs, that there will be a positive response. The hope is that being open with each other can build close relationships. This mother tried to encourage her children's involvement in her care because she knew the joy that comes from gifting someone in need with attention and care. She was wise enough to know that later, when her children experienced their own hard times, they would remember with regret their missed opportunity to reach out. Unlike the woman in the hospital who focused on her friends' wrongs, she simply filled herself with gratitude for the friends and husband who did stand by her side.

I am sure you remember times you missed the mark with your support or care for someone. Maybe you wonder if you should do something to make up for your failure. A young woman shared she was buffaloed as to what to do on her parents' fiftieth anniversary, which was a year after her father's death. She did nothing. She made no acknowledgment of the special day. I asked, "Do you believe your mother was hurting on that day?" She answered softly, "Yes." So I assured the daughter that a vase of flowers and a note, even late, would feel like a hug and an apology. I hoped the daughter's acknowledgment of her concern on her parents' anniversary would be appreciated—and, if not, at least it eased the daughter's guilt for not sharing a hug on such an important occasion. It is experience that grows empathy.

No one can comprehend what someone who has undergone tragedy, intense hurt, disease, or loss needs unless those needs are communicated. Even those who have walked a similar path may hesitate to reach out for fear of a negative reaction. Be honest with friends and family, allowing them to walk beside you. It is a dishonor to others if they watch you seemingly soar through tragedy as if it were merely a nuisance in your life. They will feel discombobulated and weak when in their own times of travail.

We were so grateful when both of our sons and their families joined us on important times after Kim's death. We knew they took time from their busy schedules because they wanted to support us at periods they knew would be difficult. We were blessed by their caring. They were hurting also. We needed to encircle each other. We had many friends and family who were incredibly caring, and some who were not. Some said, as time passed, "I wanted to help, but I just didn't know what to do." We understood because of the many times we, too, had not reached out to those in need. Life is a teacher.

Be Careful of the Ws

Sharing is not the problem for many of us; rather, it is being wise with the four Ws—when, where, with whom, and what to say—and knowing the rules of how-to. It is difficult to think through such basic fundamentals when your inner being is in a whirl of chaos. Write the Ws and your plan on how to address them in your journal when you are in a time of woe. As you review it periodically, you may recognize your progress in recalibrating as time passes.

Let's think through them together.

When?

Share at appropriate times, but do use discretion. If you feel the time is opportune to remember someone or the injustice, do so. Don't worry about what is the *right time for someone else*; what is the *need-time for you*? I have listened to many complain that when their loved one died, or they were in the midst of crisis, friends acted as if that individual had never existed or the problem was unimportant. Remember, until you open the door, most will not even knock. Be warned, however: our society expects the fallen to stand back up, regardless of the blow. The more time that passes after the catastrophe, the less another is willing to tolerate your suffering.

A woman told of the first family reunion after her father's death. He was the beacon in her life and the stalwart guard of their extended family. No one mentioned her father's name. She didn't want to be thought a whiner, so she also said nothing though her father was a constant thought. Sad. She failed to talk about her need because of fear of being labeled weak, so instead she harbored hurt and anger! How much better if she had simply commented, "I am certainly missing my father." I imagine many of the family were also missing him but were awaiting her signal that she welcomed their memories.

Where?

Be respectful of the situation. Suitable statements at appropriate times are fitting. Timing is as important as presentation. It is distracting to bring up distressful concerns in the midst of a celebration, concert, or any other focused event. Yet if jazz concerts were your deceased husband's favorite time to be with friends, remember him while at a concert with a comment such as, "Wouldn't Rob have loved this music! We all had such a good time at these events!" Friends and family hurt, too, and your simple, in-context statement allows them to open up and affirm a positive memory. In-depth conversations need an appropriate location where emotions and concerns can be expressed without distracting from the reason for the get-together.

With whom?

There is an old adage: *if you want a friend, ask for help.* Those with whom you share your concerns and whom you ask for advice become invested in you. They will listen to you cry or rage without defining you as a donkey or wimp. If your travail intensifies with time, seek a professional counselor, a pastor, or a wise friend for an outside perspective.

You may need medical help or more intensive therapy through group counseling or even an inpatient facility. If so, laugh at the irony of being without privacy and sharing your woe with total strangers. It is a perfect scenario! You have a sounding board in a group setting with fellow seekers who are too wrapped around their own concerns to worry about or remember your problems. Those who love you can remain prayerful and expectant that this time in a controlled counseling situation is precious, well-spent time!

Sharing is not the problem for many of us; it is being wise with the Ws—when, where, with whom, and what to say.

Importantly, do not forget that prayer is a universal remedy and a way to share your feelings with God, who loves you, regardless of the time of day or night.

What to say?

Few need to know every detail of your adversity. To an acquaintance, a simple, "This is a tough journey" allows those who care to know your state of being without giving details. "I appreciate your concern" is an appropriate response to advice. If more is needed, suggest you will consider their recommendation. Keep in mind that the person making a suggestion wants to help you find your way to happiness again.

If someone is insistent that you follow their recommendation, they may feel the same as a physician who knows his patient is choosing a generic medication because of insurance coverage. He knows his recommended state-of-the-art medication has broader coverage range and a faster resolution. If the patient recovers, the physician may applaud but will probably never think it was the better choice. Likewise, your friend may believe you chose a more difficult path, but does it matter? Your goal is recovery, not affirmation.

Tying It Together

One of the greatest gifts of life is friendship. Treasure friends who support you as you struggle to find your way; forgive the ones who fail. The mantra is simple: if you are hurting, ask for help. Believe me, walking with a friend in the dark is better than walking alone in the light.

LIFELINES

1. Appreciating what a family member or friend can give, instead of focusing on what they fail to do, makes life much sweeter.

2. No one can comprehend what someone else needs unless those needs are communicated.

3. Empathy and caring grow through experience.

4. Sharing may not be your problem; it is being wise with the Ws—when, where, with whom, and what to say.

5. The friend who holds your hand and says the wrong thing is made of dearer stuff than the one who stays away.

15

Seek Your Purpose

The two greatest days of your life are the day you are born and the day you find out why.

Mark Twain

■ **ANCHOR: I seek ways to find the good that comes from my experience.**

Undoubtedly one of the most important tools for overcoming personal anguish is to reach out to others with care. It may seem a bit counterintuitive to help someone else when you are hurting. Still, the reality is that when you do, though it may help the other person, it surely helps you more.

Though no one welcomes serious problems, such times often plant the seeds of why we are here, our heartbeat purpose. Recognizing a need or feeling called to a cause in such times may be the good that comes from experiencing the bad. But don't expect

149

to recognize *purpose* overnight. In fact, you probably felt scalded when someone made an insensitive comment such as, "This will make you stronger!" or "You'll be a better person after this hard time!" But ultimately, as we deal with what is, we find a need for justification of such anguish.

I remember reading every book I could find on recovery with the hopes of finding some key to keep my family together after LeeAnne's death. I read books on recovery after divorce, serious health issues, addiction, and toxic relationships but there simply were no books that helped me understand the intensity of my feelings.

Book learning and experience are often two different arenas! I had taught courses on death and dying and yet experiencing the death of a child affirmed that I was a novice. I knew the stages of grief but had no appreciation of the bounce-phenomenon—bouncing from one stage to another and back again—denial, bargaining, anger, depression, acceptance. I was here today and there tomorrow. I found the intensity of grief to be beyond survivable. How were we to find the way back from longing for what was no more?

I began to write. A book was needed, not a book about my wonderful child but rather a book about survival after tragedy, coping techniques, and help for caregivers. Though I had never written a book before, I did not question that the manuscript would be published. The market for such a book was barely tapped, a coup for a publishing firm. Plus, I had the psychology background and the firsthand experience needed to provide a guide that might help families and caregivers.

I sent the finished manuscript to ten companies with a game plan in my mind. I would fly to New York to secure a ghostwriter to tidy up the book and an agent to push it, if it were rejected by all. Fortunately the manuscript was accepted by Revell, the most prestigious Christian publishing house. The point is: *I felt purpose driven*. I wanted to help families who, like mine, were struggling to survive. I had little experience in writing a book but I was driven to do so. Reaching out to help others understand what they are experiencing is a drive within my spirit and a cause I never would have considered if I had not experienced such a tragedy. It is a gift that assuages the pain.

I have spoken in grief recovery groups throughout the country. Those of us who have experienced an emotional tsunami travel the same path. Our emotions play the same tune when dealing with catastrophe. The tools that help families whose child dies are the same as those that help individuals who experience any significant devastating life change such as divorce or loss of their job—tweaked, of course, to fit each situation.

Your spirit smothers in self-pity but mushrooms with a sense of purpose.

Make certain you are running *toward* something, not running *from* something as you seek to reverse the downward spiral of your catastrophe. When life is turned topsy-turvy it is normal to seek something different, new, and *away*. It feels like the only right direction is "not here." This is a time to be especially thoughtful of the road you take. A good general rule is not to make any major change the first year while you are adjusting to the already spinning chaos—no move to a different location, no relationship or job change. Wait until the dust settles before you shift course.

As healing slowly takes place, we recognize we are changed. Our priorities reset. It is no longer just about "me." Life becomes more about *giving* than taking and *caring* than *wanting*. It becomes more about living a *significant life* than merely having a *fun life*. We want our time to count. We begin to discern that reaching out to others to help them along their journey lights the darkness for two—the one you help and yourself.

Focusing on others takes your eyes off your belly button. You recognize your story, the insights you have gleaned, and your new knowledge of how to recalibrate may help not only you but also another person struggling along the way. You find purpose that flows from the suffering you have endured. You are emboldened with a confidence born from surviving and a faith that is simple. Joy flows as you see good coming from your experience. You discover the world is bigger than your problem or your pain. Your spirit mushrooms with a sense of purpose.

Be very aware that you must balance your needs with your outreach to others. *Self-focus* is critical to determine what is most important for your life after you suffer a setback. It isn't necessary to jump ship, give up on a goal, or throw away past relationships. But you do need to evaluate your priorities, determining what *is* most important to you, not what *was* most important. What do you enjoy *now*? Whose company encourages you *now*? You must care for others *even as you care for yourself*. That means you must balance helping others with fulfilling your needs. Care for others that is birthed by guilt and penance is unhealthy.

Helping someone also helps the one who offers care.

Care for yourself was probably the last concern on your mind in the early months following your world being torn apart. But now, as you feel more balanced, you need to care for you. When you are fit, in good health, and make a point of looking your best, you will feel more confident and able to handle your stress. This is different, of course, from comparing your looks to others. It's about being comfortable with *you*. You will be more able and wise in reaching out to others if you are balancing other-focus with self-focus.

Being involved in the lives of others, sharing *you*, where you are with what you have, may literally save your life. A general told of an encounter of his Marine Corps Reserve troop who paused from their mission to help a group of children suffering from hunger and cold. The soldiers gave the children food and warm jackets. One of the boys whispered to a corpsman that an ambush ahead would attack the troop. The willingness of the troop to reach out to the kids probably saved their lives. Your outreach may do the same for you.

Heal by Helping Others

Tragedy and woe put us on a journey. In the beginning there is confusion. We are stymied, quaking, and unable. The emotions fight. But so often as we look back we appreciate how the challenges we met opened opportunities for us to be useful in ways we never imagined. It is difficult to believe that good can come from a tragedy, such as befell actor Christopher Reeve. He was thrown from a horse during an equestrian competition in Culpeper, Virginia. Quadriplegic, he required a wheelchair to move and a portable ventilator to breathe for the rest of his life. It was striving to find purpose in his suffering that spurred Reeve's courage—and advanced paralysis research. He lobbied on behalf of people with spinal cord injuries and cofounded the Reeve-Irvine Research Center, whose discoveries offer hope to thousands of paralyzed patients. Fulfillment and a sense of purpose often sneak in an unexpected door.

Fulfillment and a sense of purpose often sneak in an unexpected door.

Izzy Paskowitz considered his life to be just peachy.[1] He was a legendary surfer in San Juan Capistrano, had a beautiful wife, Danielle, and loyal and spirited friends. But "peachy" changed after the birth of Izzy's first child, Isaiah. Isaiah is autistic, and not the high-function autism labeled Asperger's. Isaiah's autism is hardcore, with nonverbal, don't-touch-me, draining behaviors that demand his parents' constant attention to quell his drumming, injuring, and screaming. Isaiah is their angel when asleep but when awake enjoins bedlam with chaos.

Izzy withdrew from surfing. He became despondent, asking himself, *What help am I to my son? What kind of life can he have? How can good come from such a mess?* He didn't have a magic wand to make his family life sparkle, nor did prayers turn the bad into good. Life became all about Isaiah and responsibility. Have you felt such dismay as the needs and responsibilities overwhelmed you?

One particularly stressful morning, Izzy took his young son to the beach to play in the sand and splash in the water. Danielle needed time free from struggling with their little guy. Amazingly, Isaiah seemed transformed in the water. He laughed and played as he paddled on a small surfboard. That time at the beach became an everyday joy. Izzy began to feel direction, a path. He dreamed of starting a surfers' day camp for Isaiah and other autistic children. The ocean was the one place life seemed back on keel.

Surfers Healing was born in 1999 with the goal to provide an outlet for children with autism as well as the parents and friends caring for them. Today Surfers Healing has camps on both the Atlantic and Pacific coasts where volunteer surfers transform lives through providing social time and fun in the water. When asked about the tragedy of having a child with a handicap, Izzy responds, "How else could I have found where my ordinary life could make such a difference?"

Productive Outreach

Using who you are to care for others is critical. If you flee or hide after a problem, you remain self-focused and the hurt moves from a mere hurricane to a perfect storm. Volunteer, offer your care, telephone to encourage—use your gifts so the possibilities emerge.

Don't be pushed by what has happened to you; let yourself be led as doors open.

A woman who had actively participated in a four-hour conference on the gifts of reaching out approached me. She listed a plethora of justifications for not involving herself with others: "I hurt, I can't hear well, I don't drive, and my writing is illegible. . . ." She did indeed have a problem: she enjoyed being a victim. Her suffering was her comfort. Unfortunately, the longer she plays the song of tragedy, the fewer will seek her company and the more at-risk she becomes for the myriad of health problems that accompany isolation. Are you reaching out to others or are you at risk?

Contrast that woman's sad life to June Barrett's. June's bright, vivacious fourteen-year-old daughter, Lori, was in a car accident that left her physically and mentally challenged. The teen was hospitalized for seven months and required round-the-clock nursing care for years. June saw firsthand the critical needs of those with traumatic brain injury (TBI) as she struggled with the issues faced by their family. She felt led to do something that would help families like hers, struggling with their loved one's needs after a brain injury. June has joined hands with thousands and worked diligently with state and federal programs to bring about a residential facility with social programs and job training for those with TBI. Today the Crumley House TBI Rehabilitative Center is world renowned.

Don't be pushed by what has happened to you; let yourself be led as doors open.

The stress of June's difficult journey has weighed heavily on her health, but regardless, June is vivacious and bubbly. She joins with many who recognize that tragedy in life often gives life significance. Of course, she would wish for Lori to be healthy and able, but she expresses with gratitude that this great tragedy in her daughter's life has gifted both June and Lori with the opportunity for their lives to make a momentous difference and offer hope to thousands.

We might ask if we use the wrong word to describe troubles. Are they gifts or opportunities for our life to be significant, as Izzy felt through his struggles with Isaiah's autism, or should we see our problems as trials that we pass or fail?

Tragedy not only changes your world; it changes you. It gives you a story to share or a cause to support. Do you know someone who rose from the tragedy in his or her life to find blessing?

- Franklin Delano Roosevelt's battle with polio's debilitating effect on his legs caused him serious depression. In his time of partial recovery in Warm Springs, Georgia, his vision and desire to help the less fortunate grew. Roosevelt, more than any other president, is responsible for our nation's social programs for the needy.

- One-third of our United States presidents lost either a mother or a father during childhood, as did half of the Parliament in England. Each of these leaders found a way from tragedy to purpose through serving others.

- Clara Barton's battle with ill health spurred her to offer nursing care to English soldiers injured in WWI. Her care opened the nursing profession to women.

- Even though Helen Keller was blind and deaf, her courage and speaking were the impetus for multiple special programs for the physically challenged.

Try these six suggestions to turn from focusing on your own problems to reaching out to others.

1. *Trust* that there is a plan for your life and the experiences of your life.

2. *Consider* that your journey gives you the opportunity to be a teacher. What insights and tools have you learned that will ease someone else's journey?

3. *Ask* yourself where your experience, gifts, talents, knowledge, and insights could make a difference.

4. *Listen* to thoughts that hint your care might help.

5. *Start* quietly by offering your help but add depth to your service by truly caring for the individual or persons.

6. *Move* with determination toward your goal of helping where you are needed, one step at a time.

No one wants bad things to happen. Still, we all will have our share of difficulties. The question is whether you will allow your life tragedy to suck the joy from your life or use the lessons gleaned from your experience to give your life depth. Using your experience to help others is a sure way to stave off the gremlins that want to rummage in the negative. Using your experience may fill you with a deep sense of joy and purpose. The good arises from the ashes of the bad.

Does the ache as your memories pop up ever completely leave? The answer is no, regardless of what you do. However, as you understand your emotions' pull, focus on the good in your life, and reach out to others, the pain's intensity dulls. You discover coping techniques to pull yourself away from focusing on your loss or injustice.

You may not be able to help everyone or do everything, but you can help someone and do something. If a surfer who loves to play in the water, a paralyzed actor, and soldiers on the battlefield can make a difference by using their crises to help others, you can use your problems and foibles to make your life meaningful and your outreach significant.

Think of the people you know whose lives seem vital and full of purpose, and I imagine you will find they overcame much. You read in their actions that each knows life is not just about "me!" You and I can do the same. You may be a retired farmer who helps 4-H club youth, an executive who gives insight to start-up businesspeople, a storyteller who shares stories with children or seniors, or a food lover who enjoys sharing a meal with someone who needs not only food but also companionship.

Use who you are to be involved in the present and change the future rather than cocoon in the past.

The tears of difficulty water either inner peace or bitterness. The choice belongs to each of us as we struggle through our crisis. I pray that you root deeply in rich soil where faith becomes simple, priorities change, and steadfast family and friends become a big chunk of your heart. Use who you are to be involved in the present and change the future rather than cocoon in the past. The world is full of suffering; it is also full of overcoming.

LIFELINES

1. Tragedy changes not only your world; it changes you.
2. The sooner you begin reaching out to others to help them along their journey, the sooner you will become like light in the darkness—for the one you help and for yourself.
3. Make sure you are running toward something, not from something.
4. Don't be pushed by what has happened to you; let yourself be led as doors open.
5. Book learning and experience are often two different arenas!
6. Fulfillment and a sense of purpose often sneak in an unexpected door.
7. Tread on, look up, and do right until a light turns on.

When You Want to Help

The best way to cheer yourself is to try to cheer somebody else up.

Mark Twain

■ **ANCHOR: I will reach out to those who need help.**

My child wouldn't do such things . . .
I don't need all that medicine . . .
He isn't having an affair . . .
I am not going to roll over and take this lying down . . .
She isn't dying . . .
It isn't true . . .

Rational thought often flees when we are in crisis. We want to help, but it isn't always easy to help someone in distress. We are often not sure what to say or do. We fear rambling and saying the wrong thing. Or worse, we do nothing, which is not only unhelpful but layers us with guilt. We must break through our fears to encourage our loved one or friend. Sometimes we must help them face their reality. Try thinking about what you would need in the situation and act accordingly.

I listened to a quiet young mother lamenting her care for her emotionally disturbed son. She was distraught as she described being out of control, yelling and shaking the lad. "I've always been able to handle difficult situations, but I am desperate," she explained. "I've tried everything and now I'm like a teapot of boiling water, steaming with the slightest bit of heat."

I understood. I felt the same anxiety when our daughter Kim was dangerously sick. I so wanted Kim to win the fight for her life. She was valiant, but still, she was losing her struggle. I was filled with fear. Both this mother and I needed to know it is normal to be anxious when chronic issues drain our reserve. Patience is weak when pressure is unending. We both needed to reach out for help. We needed time away to recoup. But time away isn't physically possible when you are in the midst of the turmoil.

My husband innately understood what was needed. As a physician he works with people every day who seek encouragement as they develop a plan for their health care. Encouragement is what our daughter Kim, the mother struggling with her son, and I needed. That is what everyone needs when we are in trouble, our health fails, our addiction controls us, our marriages skew, our children stray, or our dreams shatter.

No one wants to give up; everyone wants to win, but sometimes the battle is too difficult, the pain too overpowering, or the struggle too hard. It is the time for those who are concerned to put care into acts that hug and encourage. *Care* and *love* are verbs that require action, not thoughts that one internalizes. Saying "I care" means little if it isn't followed by considerate action.

My husband and I teach a class on death and dying at Quillen Medical School. Most of the students are new to the experience of serious health issues or death, yet by their junior year they must begin to voice death announcements or diagnose ill health to a family. Some hit and run. Others seem like a deer in the headlights. All the students seek direction. Paul and I understand what they need because we stand on both sides of the track, the medical side and the patient and family side.

The Family Side

The physicians who cared for LeeAnne and Kim were personal friends who were concerned that we become realistic about our daughters' critical conditions. I assure you that my husband and I did not believe either of our daughters would die, regardless of their prognosis or our life in the medical world. Like anyone else would do, we saw what we hoped for, not reality. Though we were, and are, grateful for each doctor's care, ultimately only one dialogue shattered our blindness when LeeAnne lay connected to life by machines. Think about each presentation. There is a point that is critical for those of us sharing our concern with others.

Counsel given too bluntly is trashed.

The neurologist addressed the issue factually. "If LeeAnne survives, she will have no cognitive brain function. She will be curled in a fetal position, unable to walk, talk, or in any way communicate." He elaborated about feeding tubes, ulcers, and round-the-clock care. He said plainly that there was no hope. My inner response: *No way! You left out our daughter's tenacity and God's design.*

Counsel given too gently slides past reality.

The neurosurgeon called Paul, who was desperately trying to see as many of his scheduled patients as possible in case LeeAnne's condition worsened. The physician said, "Paul, things don't look good." Paul's inner response: *Lee isn't getting better. I must hurry. Faster.*

Counsel that partners has the best hope of awakening to reality and launching a plan.

Our pediatrician Dr. Boyce Berry's presentation of the same facts alerted us to bring our daughter Kim home from college so the family could be together to surround LeeAnne before the life-saving machines no longer held her to life. He sat with me in the wee morning hours, chitchatted a moment, and then, with tears in his eyes, he said, "Betty, I haven't been able to sleep. I've studied every option and I don't see anything else that can be done. I think the time is short. Let's discuss the options so you and Paul can think through critical decisions." My inner response: *We must be realistic or we will be filled with regret.*

The Caregiver Side

Catastrophe blinds you. You don't believe the worst will happen until it does. You know anything is possible, but not at this moment, not right now. So if you see someone careening down the mountain toward a cliff, step up to the challenge. You don't have to have all the answers. Do not bludgeon hope, but don't skirt the issue either. Do encourage the individual to make critical decisions that may prevent years of regret.

There are a few steps that open the ears of those who are stymied by their catastrophe.

Begin by asking for the person's understanding of the problem.

The director of St. Jude's Children's Hospital sought my help. His team of nurses was distraught over a recent patient's death. A twelve-year-old child with leukemia was brought to the hospital by his father. The father helped his son settle into his hospital room and then left him in the care of the nurse on duty. The nurse pleaded with the father to wait until the physician arrived. He left, assuring her he would return after his team's baseball game. The child died before his return. The nurses were troubled. What kind of father leaves his child to die with strangers while he plays ball?

I wanted to help, but how? I began by asking the nurses to tell me about the family. There were several factors that put the whole family at risk, not just the deceased child:

- The father's new job was a career change.
- The family had moved from their home seven hundred miles away to our community within that year.
- The deceased child had three younger siblings, the youngest a newborn baby.
- The mother was in postpartum depression.
- That twelve-year-old son had been hospitalized multiple times during his three-year struggle with chronic leukemia.

How was the family? New job. New community. New baby. Chronically sick child. They were stressed, lonely, and tired. Why was the father playing baseball? Did he need a window of relief so he could handle his family's needs? Was he attempting to develop friendships for a circle of support?

The nurses had every right to be upset. The child's death was tragic. But caregivers must see the bigger picture. No patient is an island. There are family and friends whose beings are tied to that person in the hospital bed. The nursing team's first concern was for the child but they also needed to care for the family—which would need to fight for its life at a time its reserves were already drained. The nurses' anger melded into sympathy.

Listen to build a bond of trust that allows you to partner.

When we honestly ask ourselves who in our life means the most to us, we recognize it is the one who, instead of giving advice, solutions, or cures, has chosen to share our pain and touch our wounds with warm, tender care. He or she listens without correction. *Listening establishes a bond of trust.*

Be ready when the moment is right to partner.

Most of us in uncertainty want a game plan, but few want to feel controlled. Offer ideas or ask questions so that any plan that emerges is owned by the one you want to help. Try comments that ask, not demand. "I wonder if this might be helpful for you?" "Rehab programs have rules, so would 'home rules' help?" "What are you offering that seems to help?"

A woman shared that her ninety-five-year-old father-in-law, Pops, flatly rejected his children's counsel to stop driving. He upped his insurance, saying, "I took care of the risk of lawsuits!" An attorney friend suggested, "Attorneys are hungry now, and it won't just be your father-in-law in jeopardy if he has an accident. It will also be his extended family." Pops was a headstrong man, but as his daughter-in-law talked with him privately about the attorney's concern, Pops paused. "Well, for the sake of my family, I'd best stop driving!" Stopping on his terms felt like an act of caring, not succumbing to old age.

You may have a similar struggle in your home: a family member who won't seek medical care, an adult child who won't search for employment, or a spouse who is bent on wrecking the family structure. The list of issues involving one person and affecting others is endless. You can't make someone change course but you can find ways to encourage better decisions for long-term good.

Give advice in a sandwich.

The sandwich method is a proven technique that opens ears to counsel. Start the sandwich with a positive comment, spread the negative concern in the middle, and end with another positive slice. For instance, let's think about the conversation with Pops.

- Positive: I know you are a wise and able man.
- Negative: I'm concerned because others may use "age" as a factor in an accident.
- Positive: I know this is a tough decision to give up something so critical, but I've always been impressed by how you put your family's well-being first.

Listening and being supportive are difficult when old negative patterns repeat. A woman who was suffering severe depression after her only child died and her marriage crumbled joined her friends for a yoga class at the gym. She did a few exercises and then sat down in the middle of the floor, legs crossed and head bowed like a whipped dog. You could feel her despair. Two friends joined her. Surely they were offering her a hand up; instead, they bluntly said, "Get up. You have sulked long enough."

Her friends' exasperation is typical of those who deal with negative behaviors that seem to have no end. Still, I guarantee the sandwich approach is a better method of counsel—not only for the one needing help but also for the one offering care.

Offer tools, not solutions.

Words are a powerful tool that pull toward a better choice or push in the wrong direction. You may be certain the answer for someone is to divorce, to give up on a recalcitrant kid, or to quit a job, but it is always better to let the individual who will bear the consequences decide what he or she is willing to live with. Try to give them tools to handle the difficulties as opposed to advice to bail. Giving up on someone is a big decision, one that may change the future for generations. Difficult relationships may be an opportunity to become a better person who is more patient, caring, and capable of loving. Other times, running is a lifesaver! Advise from logic, not as a reaction to emotional drama, whatever the problem.

Advice should come from rational logic, not as a reaction to emotional drama.

Here are some simple guidelines.

- *Be up front.* "I am here because I care and you need help."
- *State your intentions.* "I am going to fix your meals until you are better."
- *Ask questions.* "Would you allow me to help?" "Would going to a clinic for a checkup be wise?"
- *Never assume the "momma" role.* "I know best!"
- *Be honest in a caring manner.* "This does not seem to be helping. Would it be helpful to . . ."
- *Mollify a discussion by laughter.* For instance, you've been told to bug out! Laugh and comment, "Surely you don't think I would leave my best friend in a crisis like this . . ."
- *If you are rebuffed, apologize but ask suggestively,* "Surely you want me to care if you are struggling. I'm here and I'm staying."
- *Be an encourager who offers hope, not statements that suggest benefits,* such as "You will find a better . . ."
- *Address the anguish.* "This is such a profound loss (or hurt) for you."
- *Make your comments specific, not by innuendo.* For example, use proper names, not "he" or "she," and name the specific

problem: "Your boss was harsh," not "Everyone who works has problems."

- *Share a happy memory.* "Your son loved watching football games with you!"
- *Be specific when you offer help.* "I will park the cars . . . mow the lawn . . ."
- *Be willing to offer counsel without expectation that it will be heeded.*

The Big No

There are three behaviors that kill one's motivation to change: *begging, nagging,* and *concern over how the person regards you.* Begging puts the power in the hands of the one you are trying to move in a different direction. It also builds walls that are thick and impenetrable. Nagging sets the determination to go in an opposite direction in concrete. Focusing on what someone will think of you when you speak candidly squelches truthfulness.

No begging allowed. No nagging allowed. No belly-button focus.

A woman asked for help. She was married to a wolf who flaunted his affairs. She whined, pleaded, begged, and crawled for his attention. "Stand up!" her counselor suggested in a dozen—hopefully tactful—ways. The husband had married someone he was attracted to because of her strength, charm, kindness, or another more nebulous trait he needed for fulfillment, not a worm crawling in the dirt. If it had been only for sex, obviously he knew how to get it without marriage.

The conversation ended with this distraught wife sharing that Casanova left for a road trip, flaunting his plans of flinging whenever with whomever. Her response? She handed him a cooler packed with goodies. She was so fearful of losing the relationship that her response was killing any hope of rebuilding their very screwed-up marriage. Begging is a death knell. If you have already shared your needs, concerns, and hopes succinctly and clearly, you are adolescent to think the relationship dynamics will change using the same old tactics.

Nagging is a lot like begging, except it is not *asking*, it is beating the drum repeatedly. Whatever the issue, if you have stated your need—better communication, more time together, whatever—back off. Trying to change a relationship or obtain justice by beating the drum only spawns earplugs. Though you may know the change would be for the best and everyone in the world agrees with you, repetition is not only unsuccessful in bringing about change but it kills the relationship. In crisis, most people are struggling to think clearly. Constructive help is focused on encouraging or protecting the individual until they can stand on their own and employ logic. Acute problems such as health issues or death require short-term support. Your help will probably be appreciated. In contrast, chronic long-term problems that flow from poor choices and behaviors are not resolved overnight. You may feel desperate as the mother of an emotionally disturbed child, but pull yourself together if you are in it for the long haul. Pick up your communication tools and get to work offering hope and encouragement or intervention. This is a time to put on your big-girl pants and hang tough! You may have to get your sense of satisfaction from knowing you are doing the right thing for the safety or care of the individual.

If you are dealing with a longtime problem, be prepared to struggle with understanding *why* people make choices that negatively affect their world—and yours. Addictions, abuse, depression—the list is endless of problems that spin off unwise behaviors or the

Saying the same old thing repeatedly spawns earplugs.

body's chemical needs that are not easily resolved. There is no right "pill" to quick-fix the problem. Seek the right intervention—mental health or medical professionals or police. You are helping because the person needs your care, not because you want to be liked. Refuse to fear that the individual will be angry. Your concern is for their safety or for the safety of those in their care. The reality is that of all the people in this world, God may have felt you had the strength to handle this problem. It is your opportunity to offer someone a chance, to make a difference, to be significant in another's life.

Support is spelled h-o-l-d-i-n-g.

In handling long-term issues:

- don't weigh what others do against your efforts,
- keep your eye on the goal,
- find ways to take a break from the responsibility, and
- be grateful for the opportunity.

Sometimes we must help the one who should cradle us. So be it! Helping others to whom we commit, especially those who should be our protectors, offers us opportunities to become more understanding, more connected, and most of all more appreciative that our ultimate support is always holding us. Each of us could share our deepest thanks for those who, when we were in a dark place, rekindled our light. Support is spelled h-o-l-d-i-n-g. Hold out your arms to hug, hold out your hands to offer help, and hold out words to encourage.

LIFELINES

1. No one responds well to being told how to do something, but most people do want a plan.

2. Care may be the *pull* that assists a better choice or the *push* that sends someone in the wrong direction.

3. Even the smallest act of caring is like a drop of water that causes ripples throughout the pond.

4. Begging puts the power in the hands of the one you are trying to move in a different direction.

5. Sometimes what is needed are tools to handle difficulties as opposed to advice to jump or bail.

6. Nagging sets determination to go in the opposite direction in concrete.

7. Saying the same old thing repeatedly spawns earplugs.

8. Be hopeful and caring without being naive.

9. If you explained, reasoned, and offered but change is not in the making, you are adolescent to think the same old tactics will bring change.

17

The Forgotten Children

It is easier to build strong children than repair broken men.

Frederick Douglass

■ **ANCHOR: I will help children understand.**

Your help is crucial when a child experiences a life upheaval. Perhaps you believe children, even older youth, are in their own world of play, too young to appreciate the significance of a family catastrophe. If so, you are in good company. Until the late 1960s, even child psychologists believed that a child would be distraught and feel unsafe when disaster broke the family's routine but would quickly bounce back to happiness when his or her world calmed and routine was reestablished. This is not true!

My son Brad was just over two years old when LeeAnne died. With my background in child psychology, I knew that as soon as our home life calmed, Brad would be fine. How wrong I was! Brad did not even begin to ask for LeeAnne until his family life seemed routine again. Then he began to periodically whine for her, asking her to come and play with him. At age three, when we would drive by her school he would wonder why we didn't stop to get her. He didn't want to go to church, because church words were wrapped around LeeAnne. Church? Heaven? God? No way. We knew he didn't understand, regardless of how many times we tried to explain—but we also recognized how important it was to keep trying to help him understand at his level of maturity.

The return to happy is as erratic for the child experiencing chaos as it is for the adult. Age changes the outward expressions birthed in hurts, but a child startles and flails even in infancy when *normal* changes. Certainly infants lack the vocabulary or understanding to identify or interpret their feelings, yet children are far more intuitive than we credit. Every parent recognizes that his or her child reads facial expressions and body language. They hear and feel anxiety, anger, and fear. Try an experiment with a toddler. Drop an object. If the child perceives the object was dropped accidently by reading body language, he will crawl to retrieve it; however, if he interprets that the item was dropped intentionally, he will ignore it.

Multiple studies of attachment disorders in children building on research by Dr. John Bowlby have been groundbreaking and have decimated the nonsense that identified children as completely self-centered and oblivious to problems affecting others. New studies shed light on a child's response to negative life situations. Children who were without support and help in understanding the crisis and their feelings developed numerous issues of attachment, separation, and loss. Psychologists concluded that children in times of crisis experience:

- fear for their security
- separation anxiety

- normal emotions of sadness, anger, guilt, shame, and despair
- impaired ability to make emotional attachments
- control issues
- fatigue
- loss of self-esteem
- pessimism
- feelings of futility

A father sought counseling for his three-year-old. He shared the family history of divorce when his daughter was two. After the divorce the mother moved to another state and made no contact with her child. The little girl played with marbles on the carpet, seemingly oblivious to our conversation as her father talked. I asked a nebulous get-to-know-you question of the dad, "Where is your dog?" The child did not look at us but answered, "My mother is in the store." The father pointed. "See? She was too young to even remember her mother and, like that, she brings her up all the time. I have explained our separation a million times. Is this behavior normal?"

Of course it was normal. The child was missing her mother just as her father's thoughts circled around his broken relationship. Emotions were plying unspoken questions in this child's mind as she tried to make sense of her situation. The child did not understand that divorce was different from other times her mother left to shop or go to work. Always she had returned home after disappearing. Why would this disappearance be different?

The challenge for adults is to appreciate *when, how,* and *what* to share with children. When is the right time to explain the difficulties, how much should be shared, and in what should the child participate? Without an explanation of the chaos, children feel alone and fantasize as to what is happening. Fear reigns. The same is true of an adult who has serious health problems but is without a medical diagnosis or prognosis. Sick, the person lodges in fear as he or she tries to figure out the problem and its resolution.

Adults in the child's world are focused on the problems, desperate to resolve the issues and needs. Patience is frayed. They may be so emotionally distraught over the crisis that involving a child seems like adding fuel to their fire. Ignored, the child acts out or withdraws, creating more stress. It may be that someone outside the family circle is needed to support and encourage the child.

A child needs reassurance that though the world feels topsy-turvy, happiness will return.

A teacher in a Florida elementary school lamented her failed opportunity and response to a six-year-old child's tragedy. The child's stepfather abused and killed the child's sister. The teacher suggested the class hug the little girl but not talk about her sister's death. She reasoned that mentioning the sister would make her sadder. She asked, "What was I thinking? Who was talking to the child? The mother was distraught, her child was dead, and the police were questioning. The extended family lived far away."

Though children experience the same emotions as adults in times of chaos, they do not have the maturity to understand their feelings. Depending upon their age, they may never have experienced or watched others cope with hard times. The more they are allowed to feel an age-appropriate part of whatever is happening, the less they fear. Be confident, a child at any stage needs the same as the more mature: reassurance.

Children need:

to know their feelings and concerns are normal;

validation that they are loved;

guidance in steering raging emotions toward acceptable behavior;

recognition that there are better ways to express the emotions than tantrums, hysteria, or withdrawal;

reassurance that though the world feels topsy-turvy, happiness will return; and

a way to feel they are able to support and comfort those within their family circle.

It is evident that some children mature more quickly than others, so that must be taken into account when defining a developmental stage. Intelligence, maturity, and emotional need are factors that affect how quickly a child moves from one stage of development to another. Let's nutshell a few of the dynamics inherent in each developmental stage that will help us guide a child when her world is falling down around her.

Understanding five basic concepts of a child's needs is an important foundation for your outreach to children in crisis.

1. Children have three stages of emotional maturity: young child (magical stage), ages 1–6 years; child (self-centered stage), ages 7–12 years; and teenager (idealistic or cynical stage), ages 13–19 years.

2. Children will move through the response to unwanted change in a similar pattern to adults but the timing, their response, and their understanding will conform to their stage of development.

3. Children who feel loved will overcome life's catastrophes.

4. Children need reassurance that life will settle and be happy again, that their emotions are normal, and that they are needed and appreciated.

5. Children need to participate in comforting and serving the needs of those who are in anguish.

The Magical Stage

Children from birth through six years old are in a magical stage of cognitive development.

- Language is confusing.
- Concepts are locked in concrete; the abstract is not understandable.
- Division between the real and imaginary world is blurred.
- Time is confusing.
- The present moment is the only understandable time.
- Bad things are devastating.
- Emotions are fluid, changeable, and fleeting.
- The sense of security is erratic.

Though children in this stage hear answers to their questions, they may not comprehend the meaning. How is it possible to understand divorce or death? Is it not the same to the child as when his parent leaves to go to work? The parent's return is magical. Your infant may have cried vehemently when you left her in the nursery. It may have taken multiple times before she began to associate your leaving her there and then your return. In his study, Bowlby stated that two-thirds of children in the magical stage who were in chaotic situations showed definite regressive behavior such as bedwetting, crying, and thumb sucking; one-fifth were plagued with night terrors; one-fourth became excessively clingy; and one-third acted out in aggressive and hyperactive behavior.[1] I find those numbers suspect. Can you imagine any child in a chaotic, changing environment who does not show definite signs of his fears? It is normal and natural that a child in times of trouble experiences erratic emotions, insecurity, and regressive behavior. I would be highly suspicious that a child who did not show such signs of her distress would in fact be emotionally detached from reality, not aware of facial and body expression, and unable to sense emotions' signals.

Talk to children on their level of understanding with uncomplicated statements and explanations. Simplify the concepts. Repeat them as often as needed without frustration. Be unafraid to be simplistic in talking about the catastrophe. No child needs to hear gory details. Avoid phrases and images that lead a child to resent God for allowing the problem or taking his parent, sibling, grandparent, or friend. The child's mind might easily equate God to the wicked wizard in fairy tales. Some young children do not want to return to church after something bad happens because they want nothing to do with God, heaven, or a world that might turn theirs topsy-turvy.

Best advice: keep it simple. Always offer hope. "You will be okay. Life will settle down. Your family loves you. God cares."

The Self-Centered Stage

Though children ages seven through twelve may experience less confusion than younger children in times that are distressing to their parents, they also have limited understanding. What can you expect of a child in this self-centered stage?

- There is more understanding of life challenges such as divorce and death.
- Abstract concepts are still confusing.
- Laws, black and white, govern behavior and relationships.
- There is little differentiation in relationships.
- Good is not always seen as victorious over evil.
- "I" is the center of a child's universe.
- Concepts of time are understood.

- Negative emotions are threatening.
- Only the most significant emotions are understood.

This middle stage of emotional development is often the most difficult. Though language is no longer confusing, unless talking in abstract concepts, the world is perceived to be black or white. There is no gray zone. You are a friend or an enemy. There is little differentiation in levels of relationship. Friends are as dear as siblings. Remember the blood sister, blood brother bond? Friendship initiates rites and secret codes. Cliques form. If a friend is hurt, the response is as intense as if a family member were hurt.

The child's world spins around "me." If something bad happens, he questions, *Am I to blame?* or *Will it happen to me?* When bad assaults the family, she questions, *Is it my fault?* There is a heightened sense of vulnerability. Good no longer triumphs over evil. Monsters hide in closets. "I" can be hurt.

A child in this stage still does not understand his emotions' range. Of course, he appreciates happy, sad, angry, and hurt, but when emotions simmer, he copes with the heightened feelings in patterns acted out in his home. If the parent handles problems by raging, withdrawing, or isolating, he will do likewise. To analyze why she is bullied, is not liked, or is failing to be perfect is not possible. Add to this a lack of understanding, self-blame, and self-centered focus—and the mix is a dangerous vulnerability to unhealthy coping mechanisms such as cutting, anorexia, bulimia, addiction, and rebellion.

A ten-year-old became withdrawn and sullen after his father was hospitalized for mental illness. His grades in school plummeted. He did not understand the intensity of his feelings, his guilt, or his anger toward his distraught mother. Just explaining to him the normalcy of his feelings was like a salve on a festering wound. Children do not understand such feelings. They swirl in guilt and anxiety.

Your sharing of insights into what to expect in times of distress might relieve unrecognized anxiety. Consider how you feel if you have aches and pains but no diagnosis. Would you feel concern, fear, irritation, and frustration? With a diagnosis there is relief. You can make a plan to handle the health issue. Simple explanations of what is normal can be enough to bring a sense of hope and lessen the insecurity inherent in change.

Children in the self-centered stage are beginning to understand death, divorce, disease, and the other negative issues of life, but they don't understand the ramifications of such problems. They are still in the moment. There is no light at the end of the tunnel. Help them understand that their feelings are normal. Let them know there is hope for a better day. Most of all, tell them repeatedly they are loved and appreciated.

The Idealistic or Cynical Stage

In the teen years, you can expect to see:

> a maturing body,
> vacillating self-esteem,
> judgment limited by lack of experience,
> the ability to differentiate relationships,
> a desire to be appreciated for uniqueness,
> an idealistic or cynical view of life, and
> a significant range of faith.

The teen years are a conflicted time when the events of the day can move from deep rifts that scar to exhilarating moments that invigorate. A teen is old enough to feel like an adult, old enough to make decisions that affect the rest of his or her life, and old enough to fall in love—yet at the same time too young to fully understand the consequences of his or her choices or make major decisions without someone else's approval. It is a period of life when one sees life through either an idealistic lens or a cynical one.

The idealistic youth trusts God will help him through his crisis. He knows the world will right itself. He is confident of strength to fight through pain. The cynical youth feels her crisis proves the world is rotten, thinks nothing makes a difference, and screams loudly, "Why care?" She shouts, "Prayer is futile!"

Neither youth will talk openly with their parents. The idealistic youth does not want to add more anxiety to his parents' suffering. The cynical youth has a multitude of reasons not to talk with the adults in her world—adults caused the problem, adults don't see the world as she does, and adults don't have any advice worth heeding. Neither understands the normalcy of their feelings. Nor do they have a sense of how long it takes for life to recalibrate.

It may be difficult to initiate a time to talk with youth who have busy schedules. Keep trying. Be available. Take the teen to a seminar on coping in difficult times. Give him or her a devotional book geared to teens and their issues. Watch movies on surviving catastrophe such as *The Maze Runner* or *Star Wars*. Follow such opportunities with discussion. Watching a movie or reading a book and following it up with discussion is an opportunity to encourage insights. Sharing stories of individuals who have overcome problems may shine hope in their darkness. No matter what we go through in life, other people have gone through the same or worse and come out stronger on the other side.

Unrelenting hard times make youths feel powerless.

Even though teens may have more insight into their emotions, they probably do not understand their intensity. Let them vent without correcting their perspective. Simple statements of your personal view, such as "I understand your point, but I see the situation differently," open them to consideration of other possibilities. Youths of either outlook need guidance. A child who sees the world through rose-colored glasses may need a bit of reality. Those who rail against conventionalism with bullheadedness need a softened stance. Be careful of describing struggle as an opportunity to grow strength, maturity, and wisdom—adult lingo. Instead, explain that overcoming obstacles develops powers that make superheroes. Superheroes do not surrender. They fight off the villains and win. So can we!

Bottom line: let your youth know that life's challenges can leave us feeling weak and hopeless. It's in such times that anyone can give up. That is the easy thing to do. To hold it together when everyone else would understand if you fell apart—that's true strength.

Picking Up the Pieces

There will be times in life when each of us is challenged, when nothing seems to be going right, when tragedy strikes—and you are left to pick up the pieces. Hard times make us feel powerless. Too often that leads to an attitude of "I can't!" The word *can't* makes strong people weak, blinds people who can see, saddens happy people, turns brave people into cowards, robs genius of its brilliance, causes rich people to think poorly, and limits the achievements of that great person living inside us all.

The family bond can strengthen in times of challenge if children are allowed to participate in comforting and serving needs. As a child helps his family cope with injury, disease, divorce, loss, natural disasters, and addiction, he can observe and imbed courage and perseverance. His sense of purpose and trust in his own ability to meet challenge grow. He learns to trust God's care as he listens to others express assurance of God's support. The gifts of time, family, and friendship are discerned. Being told his hugs or efforts are appreciated shifts his focus from fears and anxieties to caring for another.

Offer your child an opportunity to get his eyes off his own problems by helping another. Encourage him to do something age-appropriate to help a friend or family member experiencing a difficult situation—text encouragement, babysit, make cookies. A teen painted a picture of a clown with tears streaming down its face for the family of his friend who was in a car accident. The painting was an outlet for the teen's sadness and a vehicle that allowed him to express his care. Ask the child what she thinks might be helpful. You will be surprised by her cunning and insight; she will feel enabled by her outreach.

Talk openly about critical choices. Children can choose to be wise when confronted by difficult choices. Recognizing they will bear the consequences of being in the wrong place, participating in harmful activities, eating unwisely, and not caring about safety may be counsel that fortifies them against potentially harmful choices.

Childhood is a time to dream. There are no brakes on the possibilities in one's imagination. But sometimes dreams crash. We fill with sorrow for the many children in our world who confront issues that cause adults to flounder. I am sorry my daughter Kim's children have been touched by tragedy in their childhood. But I have no doubt that though they will struggle and question, just as you and I, they will come through the scourge of sorrow with a maturity far beyond their chronological age because of their courage, faith, and caring family. Hard times are an opportunity to trust God, deepen empathy for others, and be filled with gratitude for the gifts in life.

Perhaps your hugs and caring words will offer the encouragement needed by a child. A youth from a children's home facility spent one Christmas with a host family. Forty years later he wrote to the family, sharing that his time with them had forged a vision of a loving home. He sent pictures of his own family and thanked them for showing him that a family could truly care for each other. It is when we go through life's challenges that vision and character are forged. During such times all of us should be reminded to:

Watch our thoughts, for they become words.
Watch our words, for they become actions.
Watch our actions, for they become habits.
Watch our habits, for they become character.
Watch our character, for it becomes our destiny.[2]

A child is watching.

LIFELINES

1. A child needs reassurance that though his or her life feels topsy-turvy, happiness will return.
2. Children have three stages of emotional development.
3. Regardless of their stage, children need insights an adult can share to understand their emotions.
4. Be prepared to address the same issues multiple times to children in the magical stage, because their experiences are too limited for them to have a long-range view of life.
5. Everyone does better when they understand what they feel.
6. Unrelenting hard times make youth feel powerless. The word *can't* is incredibly destructive; help the youth feel capable and able.
7. Understanding the negative and positive power of "choice" is crucial in the teen years.
8. You can't always be in control of what happens, but you are in control of your response to what happened.

18

You Will Get Through This

If there is meaning in life at all, then there must be meaning in suffering.

Viktor E. Frankl

■ **ANCHOR: I will get up and get going!**

No one asks for troubles, though I remember someone telling me her mother had prayed for her to face difficulties. I wondered why. Bad mother? No, now I know! The mother had hopeful confidence her daughter would walk through trouble with grace as she learned to trust God's care and appreciate the gift of friends and family. However, what if the daughter gave up and sank in the mire? Trouble changes you—and not always for the better.

I am grateful for the gift of adversity in my life. Would I ask for it? No way! Would I seek it for my children? No, thank you. I think everyone has their share without asking for more. Still, I am grateful for the insight and understanding forged from walking through the fire. I felt God holding me when I could not stand. I learned the preciousness of each moment and each hug. I garnered insights to share with others on their journey. I learned to walk quietly through my experiences, being grateful for the good and learning from the bad and sad.

There is Russian folklore of a little firebird named Challenge. He loved to tiptoe on the rooftops and fly in the trees. But when the clouds would come, he would fly to his mother and ask, "Why does God let the clouds take the sun away?" His mother would simply smile and say, "Challenge, one day you will see," and off she would fly. Over and over, as the clouds would return, Challenge would fly back to his mother to repeat his question.

Then one day her answer was different. She softly chirped, "Challenge, you are strong enough now. Fly through the clouds and you will see." So the young firebird determined to go through the darkness and find the sun. But the winds were strong and the rain was pelting. He was afraid and thought to turn back, when suddenly the clouds parted. He flew through the opening and there it was—the sun. The sun was always there.

Are we, like the little firebird, afraid and unable, wanting God to give us back our happiness when hurts blind us to His infinite care? Some days I am unable. Some days the memories flood and the longing is intense. The clouds cover the sun, but I know He is there. Most importantly, I know He is holding me, giving me the strength to flutter my wings.

Hope may feel far away to you when the world seems dark and cold, just as it did to the little bird. But hope is like the small hole in the dark clouds that streams light to the earth. It is like the glistening snow after a blizzard. It comes from knowing you are safe and never alone. It depends upon your sheer refusal to succumb to whatever wants to end your flight. Hope within assures you that though things will change, change can be good—maybe even better.

No one expects you to be vivacious and bubbly when overwhelmed by troubles. In fact, most would think something was wrong if you appeared to be unaware of the seriousness of your travail. It is okay to feel sad and scared. Moments of doubt, confusion, and uncertainty help us recognize that we need more than our own strength to journey through life. Hillary Clinton was right: it takes a village. But without trusting God's infinite care, even a village is not enough.

Our emotional strength and resilience, like our muscles, are built gradually with repeated exposure to obstacles. If you lack practice in confronting obstacles (as when you choose to avoid them or allow others to protect you from meeting them), a traumatic event can take you down. The struggle to stand back up is all the more difficult. Being honest, allowing family and friends to be your support, praying, and taking one step at a time will help you come through this difficult time. You can get happy in the same skin you get sad in. Our hope is to not let a bad experience make us feel like we have a bad life.

You can get happy in the same skin you get sad in.

"If you can't fly, then run. If you can't run, then walk. If you can't walk, then crawl, but whatever you do you have to keep moving forward," is the advice of Martin Luther King Jr.[1] His struggle brought significant change to our country. Think of those you know and those in history who have struggled as they fought to overcome a challenge. They became courageous and self-assured. The experience changed each person from seeing just his or her own problems to caring for others.

You have a story to share. The struggle that is so daunting for you will change you. It will assign you credence that others beginning their journey will seek. Put yourself out there! Caring, reaching out, and helping others do more than just build confidence. They take your eyes off your own problems and, instead, affirm that your difficulties serve a purpose.

I watched a news reporter interview parents the morning after the home fire that killed their five children. The couple seemed blasé about the loss, commenting they had lots of nieces and nephews to love, so all would be fine. The following year I was the speaker for a conference on grief that the couple attended. They wept throughout the program. At the session's end I came to them, but their walls came up. Their comments showed no indication of their pain. They were unable to allow others in for comfort and support. The next year I addressed the same group. This time the mother was present but not the father. She seemed a skeleton; a death mask covered her countenance. Her life—not just her happiness—was in jeopardy. She had no anchors to keep her steady in the storm. She had built walls that imprisoned her. Are you doing the same?

A Pilgrimage

Rocamadour, France, is a medieval city and pilgrimage site visited through the centuries by kings, popes, Crusaders, and pilgrims, and today has 1.6 million visitors per year. The city is carved out of the rocky crevices of a canyon below the spectacular, thousand-year-old Basilica of St. Saveur perched at the mountain's peak. On one of the rocky crevices is a memorial plaque to pilgrims who have traveled the many miles from their homes, forded the rivers, trudged through the canyons, climbed the rocky terrain, and finally ended their journey by climbing on their knees the 216 steps to the abbey. The plaque states the obvious: *pilgrimages are not easy*.

I was wandering the village street and marveling at antiquity when in the sky there was such a clatter. Two crows were attacking an eagle. The eagle was diving, trying to avert the feisty, bothersome birds. He seemed frantic. Here was a bird known as a king in the bird kingdom, powerful, worthy of fear by his subjects, acting as if he were an underdog. I shouted, "Eagle, stop ducking! You are a king. Use your talons."

Perhaps you have been ducking from God, angry that you are hurt. The journey has been difficult. But you are a child of God. Your worth doesn't come from a problem-free life. It is not to be judged by children gone astray, marriages failed, jobs lost, ill health, or voices that bully. It is dependent upon your trusting that even the struggles in your life can be overcome. Standing when the world has fallen down around you is possible because—broken, longing, and struggling—you trust God's care.

Each of us is on a pilgrimage that requires courage and tenacity to climb through the challenges and end at the summit. As you look back it may seem too much time was wasted hanging on to hurts or clinging to what could not be changed. You wonder why you did not simply pause to relish each good moment. Hopefully, instead of layering yourself with regret over wrong choices, you recognize that you were learning and growing, finding your way— and in the process recognizing God's hand guiding your discovery of what is truly valuable.

The Japanese, who mend broken objects by filling the cracks with gold, appreciate that when something suffers damage and has a history, it becomes more valuable. I have no doubt that you will become more precious as you prevail over life's challenges, because each challenge overcome gifts you with more insight and stamina and draws you into closer relationship with your Father.

When you need encouragement, cling to the anchors.

- Grab the lifelines that are anchors in the storm.
- Know that you have been training all your life to win.
- Refuse to be destroyed by your life challenges.

- Give thanks for the pain.
- Seek knowledge of what to expect in times of hurt.
- Respect anger, use it carefully, and let it go.
- Face guilt, own it, make amends, and learn from it.
- Deal with reality truthfully.
- Counter negative thoughts.
- Forgive so a wrong in the past does not imprison you in the present.
- Believe that something good can come from such bad.
- Be grateful for memory's pop-ups.
- Trust God has a plan for your life.
- Listen to the voice speaking within you.
- Let others know *what helps* and *what does not.*
- Share your lessons learned as you journeyed through hurt.
- Help children understand.
- Get up and get going.

My journey has not been easy—nor has yours. Our struggles may be different but they all lead us through the same course of emotions and decisions. Some days you simply weep. Some days loss rips your heart from your being. Some days injustice scalds your every fiber. Still, all days are an incredible blessing. Each moment is a gift to be treasured. How fortunate I am to know the extremes of joy and pain. Trusting I am where I am supposed to be fills me with an abiding joy.

In the Bible, Solomon prayed for wisdom. I doubt he understood its cost. This successful, wealthy, and powerful king learned he couldn't find joy in his own strength. Joy grows in struggle as we begin to value the treasures of friendship and caring. It is kept alive by hope from the voice within that encourages you onward. It fills you with peace when you recognize you can stand because you are held by God's hand. Solomon had to learn to be happy and to trust God's care when times were good and when times were difficult. That is wisdom. Wisdom is choosing joy in all circumstances.

"What day is it? It's today," squeaked Piglet. *"My favorite day," said Pooh.*
—A. A. Milne

Standing up when your world has fallen down around you is a decision you make to refuse to be destroyed by the hurt, to seek the gifts, and to reach out to others with your new understanding. Our greatest life messages and most significant outreach will come out of our deepest hurts. Stand up. Spread your wings! Catch the wind. Fly! You have a story to share that offers hope, a cause to lead, and lives to touch. There is no time to waste!

LIFELINES

1. The sun is always there.

2. You can get happy in the same skin you get sad in.

3. Happiness doesn't flow from a problem-free life; it comes from spreading your wings, catching the wind, and flying—regardless of your woes.

4. You are more beautiful and valuable because you have journeyed through tough times.

5. Difficulties give you a story to share that offers hope to others on their journeys.

6. Life is a pilgrimage—and pilgrimages are never easy.

Questions for Discussion

Chapter 1: Standing Up

1. Are you overcome by a problem now?
2. How is it affecting your mind, body, and spirit?
3. Do you know someone who has weathered their difficulty with grace?
4. What did he or she do that seemed different from another who wears woe as if it is a badge of courage?

Chapter 2: Facing Your Giant

1. What giant are you fighting?
2. What have you fought in the past?
3. What strategies did you use to win when coping with each?
4. Do you find similarities in the strategies, even though the battles were different problems?
5. What lifelines would you suggest to others who are facing life-shattering problems?

Chapter 3: Finding Your Way

1. What has caused you to feel joyless?

2. Are you consumed by negative thoughts and feelings?

3. Have you set realistic goals that are best for the long term?

4. Do you keep your goals first and foremost when dealing with your difficulties?

5. Do you feel anything good has come from your struggle?

Chapter 4: When Pain Is a Good Thing

1. Why could pain be a good thing in someone's life?

2. Have you had a problem that made you physically sick?

3. Does pain cause us to discern and prioritize what is valuable? Explain.

4. What good could possibly come from the pain you are experiencing?

5. Have you found ways to counter the emotions that want to suck you into anguish, rage, and shame?

6. Is it possible that the very things that cause us emotional hurt are critical to our spiritual development?

Chapter 5: Redirecting Your Thoughts and Your Emotions

1. Do you recognize how much control you have over your emotions?

2. How do you keep from locking into your negative memories?

3. Do you pray for help to find positive ways to counter negative thoughts?

4. Are you swirling around a negative event?

5. Are you allowing those who care to support you in ways that counter your negative feelings rather than turning your negative thoughts into gossip sessions?

6. Are you trying to change negative patterns established in childhood that allowed rampant emotions to control your actions?

Chapter 6: Handling the Bully

1. Are you experiencing unexpected anger?

2. Do you simmer over issues?

3. Have you talked with anyone about your feelings?

4. Do your feelings of anger cause you to rage, dislike yourself, or feel depressed?

5. How are you seeking resolution and compromise in difficult situations?

6. Has your desire for justice morphed into a need for revenge?

7. Do you have a plan to control your reaction to wrongs without denying them?

8. Have you prayed about the anger you feel and the ways you try to resolve the issue?

Chapter 7: The Elephant in the Room

1. Are you doing something that makes you feel guilty?

2. Is the guilt justified, or merely because you feel you failed at being perfect?

3. Are your negative feelings affecting your health?

4. Why could guilt be considered a gift?

5. What is the difference between guilt and shame?

6. Have you handled guilt by using it to make amends and change?

Chapter 8: When Problems Stack

1. Why do you think so many of us fight against change?

2. Do you adapt easily to change? If so, what are your secrets?

3. Have you made rapid decisions in a time of life challenge that made your recovery more difficult?

4. Why is clear thinking so difficult in the midst of problems?

5. How is it possible to be realistic about difficulties without becoming driven by feelings of doom?

Chapter 9: The Stories You Believe

1. Think about the stories you tell yourself. Are they positive?

2. Do your stories affirm your ability to handle problems? Give an example.

3. Do your stories affirm God's care? Share your thoughts.

4. Are the stories you tell spinning around a negative interpretation of the situation?

5. How have the stories you tell yourself about a family member affected your relationship? Explain.

6. Have you successfully changed a negative story about someone or an experience? How did you do it?

Chapter 10: Coping with the Pop-Ups

1. Do negative memories pop up in your thoughts?

2. How do you rid the hurt flowing from those thoughts?

3. Do you encourage warm-fuzzy pop-ups?

Chapter 11: Where Faith and Life Meet

1. Have you talked to God about your concerns, fears, and desires?

2. Have you felt God's care when journeying through a difficult time?

3. Are you afraid to tell God your needs?

4. Do you read Scripture's stories of real people—some who made it through their struggle with a deeper faith and some who turned away from their belief in a caring God? What insights have you gleaned? Explain.

5. Do you journal the times you feel God's care and encouragement?

6. Have you felt someone's outreach to you was more than coincidental? Share your experience.

Chapter 12: The Help beyond Understanding

1. Share a time you sensed the path you should take.

2. Have you experienced a sudden knowledge, dreamed a future event, or felt an urge or leading to do something unexpected?

3. Has someone called you or done something just at the moment you needed his or her care?

4. Have you felt an inner urge that argued against an action?

Chapter 13: Letting It Go

1. Who benefits from forgiving a wrong or injustice?

2. Why is forgiving so difficult?

3. How would our relationships be different if we forgave the wrongs?

4. How does trying to forget, as opposed to forgiving, cause bitterness, anger, and hurt to form stones in our heart?

5. What are indications of your personal need to forgive?

6. What does an unforgiving spirit do to the one who refuses to let it go?

Chapter 14: Dealing with Family and Friends

1. Have you found supportive care to help you through your travail?

2. Are you open about your needs with those who care?

3. Has someone done or said something that added fuel to your distress? How did you handle it?

4. What insights could you share with others to help them on their journeys?

5. Have you found prayer helpful? Explain.

Chapter 15: Seek Your Purpose

1. Are you wondering if you can ever find happiness again after whatever has befallen you?

2. Describe someone who seemed to grow kinder and wiser after his or her difficulty.

3. Describe someone who has withered after tragedy.

4. What do you think made the difference in each of their efforts to recover?

5. Has someone helped you find balance in a difficult time?

6. What have you learned as you traveled through your hurt that might help others on their journeys?

Chapter 16: When You Want to Help

1. What have you found to be helpful when you share your concern or advice with another?

2. Have you found it helpful to share your own story when reaching out to someone in a similar distress?

3. Are you nagging or begging in your attempt to bring about positive change? If so, what has been the effect?

4. Is there someone who should cradle you but rather is needy? Are you able to turn from expecting care to giving it?

Chapter 17: The Forgotten Children

1. Have you talked with your children at appropriate times about the emotions they feel?

2. Do you encourage a child in travail to discuss his or her feelings?

3. Do you appreciate how children's psychological development affects their understanding?

4. What ways have you helped a child express his or her feelings—drawings, service . . . ?

5. Do you counter a child's unspoken guilt by affirming his or her good qualities and acts?

6. Do you allow your children to be part of helping the family during the period of change?

Chapter 18: You Will Get Through This

1. Where are you on your journey?

2. Are you discovering unrecognized inner strength in your handling of your challenge?

3. Do you feel able to help someone in his or her own time of need?

4. Are you using lifelines and anchors to help you reach for possibilities, as opposed to longing for what is no more?

5. Are you afraid life will never be happy again?

6. What are you doing that is generating a sense of hope?

7. Are you praying to break through the clouds to find the sun?

Amy's Letter

My sister Amy was at work when she suddenly felt compelled to visit my daughter Kim, and she drove to Kim's home, an hour away. Amy did not know Kim would depart this life the morning after their time together. Paul and I felt she answered a call to be God's hands and His voice of comfort and encouragement.

Perhaps you are feeling such an urge to reach out to someone. Answer the call. You may discover your outreach makes a significant difference in someone's life. We were comforted by Amy's letter to us, written three days after Kim's death, that told of her time with Kim.

Lord,

All I can say is thank You for sending me to her—for allowing me to be there and be Your arms, hands, ears, words, and love to her before she left us. Thank You for letting her have a "good day," knowing she was loved, beautiful, and contributed before she left us.

Thank You for letting me tell her You loved her. Thank You for letting me hold her and love her, rub her back, and tell her she was beautiful. Thank You that I saw in her eyes that she received that love.

Thank You that she was able to share her fears and her despair, and ask for prayer. Thank You that I affirmed her hard work to try and overcome. . . . Thank You for letting me hear how much she loved You. Thank You for the friends who loved her and supported her in her struggle. Thank You for the Beth Moore Bible study she attended and the yoga she tried to do to stay spiritually and physically healthy. Lord, thank You that in all of her weakness and the enemy's power over her flesh, she was strong in her spirit. Her love and faith in You did not waver and You were always with her in her heart and spirit—and she knew that.

Thank You for letting me tell the spirit of despair to leave and command him to let her go. . . . Thank You for letting us pray together and ask angels to fill her house, to surround her, to stay with her and keep the enemy at bay. Thank You for letting me be there to ask hope and peace to fill her, and for her to feel Your presence.

Thank You for letting her remember the good times with Greg and her trip to Bora Bora. I see her smile as she recalled those memories on the kayak and swimming each morning as they woke. I hear her laughing as she saw the "wedding" in her mind's eye that she planned while she was battling the leukemia drugs and hormone imbalances, almost at death's door. Thank You for letting me be there with her on that day as well. . . . Thank You for giving her the opportunity to speak of Lauren, Ashley, Michael, and Kaylee, reliving how proud she was of each one and how she knew they would go far in life. How pleased she was that Lauren is happy and "thriving" at college . . . that Ashley can do anything with her God-given gifts . . . that Michael is bright and athletic and such a joy, and that her little Kaylee is a princess, a bubble of life. . . .

Thank You for giving me the opportunity to tell her that she was in each one of her children and how You would always care for them. She loved them desperately and wonderfully, and she wanted to be there for them and was sad when she had not been. I reminded her of what a great mom she was and the life and memories she had given each of them. Lord, thank You for letting us talk about forgiveness, letting go, and Your bringing healing.

Thank You for letting me hear her say that she did not want to go anywhere again for treatment. She was adamant! She was tired and she only wanted to stay home. It was her choice. She was firm about that and told me she had told Greg, "I am not going anywhere."

Thank You, Lord, for letting me take her for her last meal and eat her favorite food—French onion soup. We ate together and talked. She wanted to catch up on her family— Bethany, Lyndsey, Adam, Josh, Brady, Mindy, and all her cousins. We went over where everyone was and what each was doing. She loved her family, her own unit "supremely," her Brown family, her extended family. She loved her church and felt very connected to Munsey. She was grateful for these gifts of support and the family and friends who were there for her. Thank You that we could share all of that together.

Father, she loved to cook and clean and make a beautiful home for Greg and her children—to decorate and create a home they came to and could enjoy. She showed me the beautiful purple pot she bought to decorate for Ashley's birthday table. She talked of Lauren's birthday, which was *this same day, and how she wanted to be there with her at her college. She had texted Lauren several times that day but she wanted to be there to hug her in person.*

Father, the last thing we did was to go to Chick-fil-A to get supper for her family. She picked each meal for her children and wanted two sandwiches for Greg. It was important that we order the healthy grilled chicken for each one. We took them home and laid each bag in the kitchen for the kids and Greg to find when they came home. She wanted to have a good meal they liked.

After all that was done, she laid down on the couch. I covered her with blankets and gave her a pillow and told her to sleep until her family came home in thirty minutes or so. She was lying peacefully asleep when I left.

Thank You for letting me see the battle she was fighting and how deeply it held her flesh—but that her spirit was not enslaved. She was in prison in a body that had been weakened by disease. Her spirit wanted free and her desire was for You, Lord. I know You allowed her to stay and gave her life as long as she wanted. I also know You said, "Come home, Kim, I'm taking you out of this pit—the battle is over—you are free—you are Mine—come home."

I know You were there with angelic forces because we had asked You to be there. She is with You. We are sad because we loved her and wanted her to overcome . . . but we are also glad she is free!

Father God, You are so good! You meet our needs at every turn. You send us those who can give Your love and share Your heart in every situation. Thank You, Jesus, I humbly say for allowing me this great privilege.

February 23, 2013

Scripture for Help in Difficult Times

We are hard pressed on every side, but not crushed; perplexed, but not in despair; persecuted, but not abandoned; struck down, but not destroyed.

2 Corinthians 4:8–9

Trust in the Lord with all your heart
and lean not on your own understanding;
in all your ways submit to him,
and he will make your paths straight.

Proverbs 3:5–6

Do not be anxious about anything, but in every situation, by prayer and petition, with thanksgiving, present your requests to God. And the peace of God, which transcends all understanding, will guard your hearts and your minds in Christ Jesus.

Philippians 4:6–7

I have come that they may have life, and have it to the full.

John 10:10

Therefore I tell you, do not worry about your life, what you will eat or drink; or about your body, what you will wear. Is not life more than food, and the body more than clothes? Look at the birds of the air; they do not sow or reap or store away in barns, and yet your heavenly Father feeds them. Are you not much more valuable than they? Can any one of you by worrying add a single hour to your life? And why do you worry about clothes? See how the flowers of the field grow. They do not labor or spin. Yet I tell you that not even Solomon in all his splendor was dressed like one of these. If that is how God clothes the grass of the field, which is here today and tomorrow is thrown into the fire, will he not much more clothe you—you of little faith? So do not worry, saying, "What shall we eat?" or "What shall we drink?" or "What shall we wear?" For . . . your heavenly Father knows that you need them.

Matthew 6:25–32

Come to me, all you who are weary and burdened, and I will give you rest. Take my yoke upon you and learn from me, for I am gentle and humble in heart, and you will find rest for your souls.

Matthew 11:28–29

Even though I walk
    through the darkest valley,
I will fear no evil,
    for you are with me;
your rod and your staff,
    they comfort me.

Psalm 23:4

Consider the ravens: They do not sow or reap, they have no storeroom or barn; yet God feeds them. And how much more valuable you are than birds! Who of you by worrying can add a single hour to your life? Since you cannot do this very little thing, why do you worry about the rest? Consider how the wild flowers grow. They do not labor or spin. Yet I tell you, not even Solomon in all his splendor was dressed like one of these. If that is how God clothes the grass of the field, which is here today, and tomorrow is thrown into the fire, how much more will he clothe you.

Luke 12:24–28

Peace I leave with you; my peace I give you. I do not give to you as the world gives. Do not let your hearts be troubled and do not be afraid.

John 14:27

Anxiety weighs down the heart,
but a kind word cheers it up.
Proverbs 12:25

When I am afraid, I put my trust in you.
Psalm 56:3

For I am convinced that neither death nor life, neither angels nor demons, neither the present nor the future, nor any powers, neither height nor depth, nor anything else in all creation, will be able to separate us from the love of God that is in Christ Jesus our Lord.

Romans 8:38–39

God is our refuge and strength,
an ever-present help in trouble.
Psalm 46:1

Ask and it will be given to you; seek and you will find; knock and the door will be opened to you.

Matthew 7:7

Quick Reference Anchors

1. I will grab the lifelines that are anchors in the storm.

2. I have been in training all my life to win!

3. I refuse to be destroyed by my life challenges!

4. I give thanks for the pain.

5. I will counter negative thoughts through gratitude for the gifts in my life, including the lessons I learn from coping with a calamity.

6. I respect anger, use it carefully, and let it go!

7. I face my guilt, own it, make amends, and learn from it.

8. I deal with reality—what is changed, what might be changed, and what will not change.

9. I will keep my stories positive by focusing on the lessons, insights, and strengths I have gained.

10. I am grateful for the warm-fuzzy pop-ups that encourage, as well as those that vacuum my mind.

11. I trust that God has a plan for my life.

12. I will listen to the voice speaking within my spirit.

13. I refuse to allow a wrong to imprison me.

14. I will let those who care know what helps and what does not.

15. I will seek ways to find the good that comes from my experience.

16. I will reach out to those who need help.

17. I will help children understand.

18. I will get up and get going!

Notes

Chapter 1 Standing Up

1. Dr. John Witty, Widowed Persons' Association Annual Meeting, Johnson City, TN, December, 2000.
2. John 10:10.

Chapter 2 Facing Your Giant

1. 1 Samuel 17:8–9.
2. C. E. Jackson, P. C. Talbert, and H. D. Caylor, "Hereditary Hyperparathyroidism," *Journal of the Indiana State Medical Association* 53 (1960): 1313–16.
3. 1 Samuel 17:42.
4. Ethan Hirsch, Jane Cuadros, and Joseph Backofen, "David's Choice: A Sling and Tactical Advantage," International Symposium on Ballistics, Jerusalem, May 21–24, 1995.
5. Rick Warren, Twitter post, 2:32 p.m., April 15, 2011, www.twitter.com /RickWarren/status/59006112120315904.

Chapter 3 Finding Your Way

1. David Pelzer, *A Child Called "It"* (Deerfield Beach, FL: HCI, 1995), 91–92.
2. David Pelzer, "Speech for Board/Staff," Holston Home for Children, Greenville, TN, October 1999.
3. Genesis 45:5–8.

Chapter 4 When Pain Is a Good Thing

1. Elizabeth B. Brown, *Sunrise Tomorrow: Coping with the Death of a Child* (Old Tappan, NJ: Fleming H. Revell, 1988), 13–14.
2. Dr. Paul Brand and Philip Yancey, *Pain: The Gift Nobody Wants* (New York: HarperCollins, 1992), 1–5.
3. Ibid., 4.

Chapter 5 Redirecting Your Thoughts and Your Emotions

1. Philippians 4:8.
2. "Dr. Caroline Leaf Breaks Down Neuroscience with the Word of God," *Stop & Think*, September 5, 2012, http://awakeningthepsyche.wordpress.com /2012/09/05/dr-caroline-leaf-breaks-down-neuroscience.
3. John Ellard, *Normal and Pathological Responses to Bereavement*, John Bowlby and Murray Parkes, eds. (New York: MSS Information Corp., 1974), 322ff.
4. Witty, Widowed Persons' Association Annual Meeting.
5. "Impotence," *Peace and Healing*, accessed March 9, 2016, www.peaceand healing.com/psychology/sexual-health/impotence.
6. Suzanne Woods Fisher, *The Heart of the Amish: Life Lessons on Peacemaking and the Power of Forgiveness* (Grand Rapids: Revell, 2015), 21.

Chapter 8 When Problems Stack

1. Elizabeth B. Brown, "Life's Flies," *The Joy Choice: Happiness Is an Inside Job* (Grand Rapids: Revell, 1994), 75–77.

Chapter 11 Where Faith and Life Meet

1. Sonia Jaspal, "Mother Teresa: An Inspiration for Social Responsibility," *Sonia Jaspal's RiskBoard*, August 28, 2010, https://soniajaspal.wordpress .com/2010/08/28/mother-teresa-an-inspiration-for-social-responsibility/.
2. John Henry, "Why Do Christians Suffer?" June 11, 2004, http://doctrine .landmarkbiblebaptist.net/suffering.html#Reasons.

Chapter 13 Letting It Go

1. Elizabeth Smart with Chris Stewart, *My Story* (New York: St. Martin's Press, 2013), 285–86.
2. Suzanne Woods Fisher, *The Heart of the Amish* (Grand Rapids: Revell, 2015), 8.

Chapter 14 Dealing with Family and Friends

1. Marian Anne Eure, "Loneliness Can Make You Sick," *About Health*, December 30, 2014, http://seniorhealth.about.com/od/mentalemotionalhealth/a /lonely.htm.

Chapter 15 Seek Your Purpose

1. "Surfers Healing—The Izzy Paskowitz Story," Vimeo, 6:23, uploaded by Gabriel Noble_TRU FILMS, July 24, 2013, https://vimeo.com/70958326.

Chapter 17 The Forgotten Children

1. John Bowlby and Murray Parkes, *Science Direct: Social Science and Medicine* vol. 5, no. 2 (1967): 101–15.

2. "Quotes about Being Strong & the Strength of the Human Will," *Keep Inspiring Me*, accessed January 28, 2016, http://www.keepinspiring.me/quotes-about-being-strong/#xzz3xK5WLRSZ.

Chapter 18 You Will Get Through This

1. "Martin Luther King Quotes," *Goodreads*, accessed March 9, 2016, www.goodreads.com/quotes/26963.

Bibliography

Archer, Jeffrey. *Kane and Abel*. Great Britain: Hodder and Stoughton, 1979.

Arthur, Kay. *Lord, Heal My Hurts*. Portland, OR: Multnomah, 1977.

Bowlby, John and Murray Parkes. *Science Direct: Social Science and Medicine* vol. 5, no. 2 (1967).

Brown, Elizabeth B. *The Joy Choice: Happiness Is an Inside Job*. Grand Rapids: Revell, 1994.

———. *Sunrise Tomorrow: Coping with the Death of a Child*. Old Tappan, NJ: Fleming H. Revell, 1988.

———. *Surviving the Loss of a Child*. Grand Rapids: Revell, 2010.

Cousins, Norman. *The Healing Heart: Antidotes to Panic and Helplessness*. New York: W. W. Norton & Co., 1983.

Dyer, Dr. Wayne W. *Real Magic: Creating Miracles in Everyday Life*. New York: HarperCollins, 1991.

Edwards, Elizabeth. *Resilience*. New York: Broadway Books, 2010.

Fisher, Suzanne Woods. *The Heart of the Amish: Life Lessons on Peacemaking and the Power of Forgiveness*. Grand Rapids: Revell, 2015.

Gladwell, Malcolm. *David and Goliath: Underdogs, Misfits, and the Art of Battling Giants*. New York: Little, Brown and Company, 2013.

Jones, E. Stanley. *Abundant Living*. Nashville: Abingdon Press, 1942.

Keay, Ike, with William Deerfield. *Child of Pain, Children of Joy*. Old Tappan, NJ: Fleming H. Revell, 1984.

Krefft, Peter. *Making Sense Out of Suffering*. Ann Arbor, MI: Servant Books, 1986.

Leaf, Dr. Caroline. *Switch On Your Brain: The Key to Peak Happiness, Thinking, and Health*. Grand Rapids: Baker Books, 2013.

———. *Who Switched Off My Brain? Controlling Toxic Thoughts and Emotions*. Nashville: Thomas Nelson, 2009.

Lucado, Max. *He Still Moves Stones*. Dallas: Word Publishing, 1993.

Luskin, Dr. Fred. *Forgive for Good: A Proven Prescription for Health and Happiness*. New York: HarperCollins, 2003.

Mace, Nancy L., MA, and Peter V. Rabins, MD, MPH. *The 36-Hour Day: A Family Guide to Caring for People Who Have Alzheimer's Disease, Related Dementias, and Memory Loss*. New York: Warner Books, 2003.

Mandino, O. G. *The Greatest Success in the World*. New York: Bantam Books, 1982.

McGee, Robert S. *The Search for Significance*. Nashville: Thomas Nelson, 2003.

Minirth, Frank B., MD, and Paul D. Meier, MD. *Happiness Is a Choice*. Grand Rapids: Baker Books, 1988.

Morell, Paul L. *Living in the Lions' Den: How to Cope with Life's Stress*. Nashville: Abingdon Press, 1992.

Niven, David, PhD. *The 100 Simple Secrets of Successful People: What Scientists Learned and How You Can Use It*. New York: HarperCollins, 2002.

Osteen, Joel. *Your Best Life Now: 7 Steps to Living at Your Full Potential*. New York: Hachette, 2004.

Patterson, Kerry, Joseph Grenney, Ron McMillan, and Al Switzler. *Critical Conversations*. New York: McGraw-Hill, 2012.

Pelzer, David. *A Child Called "It": One Child's Courage to Survive*. Deerfield Beach, FL: Health Communications, Inc., 1995.

Schuller, Robert. *The Be Happy Attitudes*. Waco, TX: Word, 1985.

Siegel, Bernie S. *Love, Medicine, and Miracles: Lessons Learned about Self-Healing from a Surgeon's Perspective with Exceptional Patients*. New York: HarperCollins, 1998.

Siegel, Bernie S., with Cynthia J. Hurn. *The Art of Healing: Uncovering Your Inner Wisdom and Potential for Self-Healing*. Novato, CA: New World Library, 2013.

Smalley, Gary, with Al Janssen. *Joy That Lasts*. Grand Rapids: Zondervan, 1988.

Smart, Elizabeth, with Chris Stewart. *My Story*. New York: St. Martin's Press, 2014.

Stearns, Ann Kaiser. *Living Through Personal Crisis*. Chicago, IL: Thomas More Press, 2010.

Taylor, Jack R. *The Key to Triumphant Living*. Nashville: Broadman Press, 1971.

Thurman, Dr. Chris. *The Lies We Believe*. Nashville: Thomas Nelson, 1989.

Westfall, John F. *Getting Past What You'll Never Get Over: Help for Dealing with Life's Hurts*. Grand Rapids: Revell, 2012.

Wilson, Ruth. *The Gift of Anger*. Wilmore, KY: Bristol Books, 1990.

Yancey, Philip. *Disappointment with God: Three Questions No One Asks*. Grand Rapids: Zondervan, 1988.

Elizabeth B. Brown is a teacher, speaker, and professional counselor. The author of the popular *Living Successfully with Screwed-Up People*, *Working Successfully with Screwed-Up People*, and *Surviving the Loss of a Child*, Brown and her husband live in Tennessee. Learn more at www.elizabethbbrown.com.

Compassionate Encouragement
Born *from* Deep Sorrow

You will find no pat answers or patronizing panaceas here—
just real words of healing from someone who has been exactly
where you are now.

A Bestseller That Continues to Change Lives and Relationships

OVER 500,000 COPIES SOLD

Living Successfully with Screwed-Up People

Elizabeth B. Brown

You can be positive—no matter who tries to bring you down. Unfortunately, the world is full of screwed-up people. But the good news is your world no longer has to revolve around them. You can stop being the victim of others and start loving life in spite of them.

Crazy co-workers stressing you out? Here's the solution.

Less stress at work can start today.
So what are you waiting for?

THERE IS LIFE—
Rewarding *and* Abundant Life—
after Heartache *and* Pain

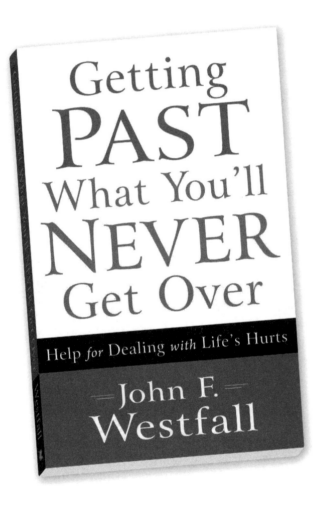

You *can* find hope and peace— no matter what.

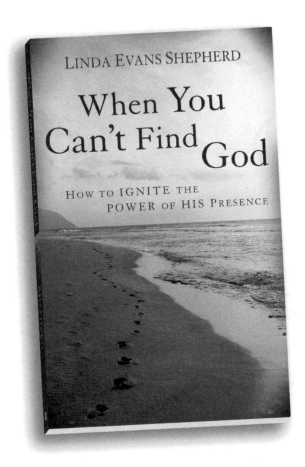

LINDA EVANS SHEPHERD teaches you how to see God in any circumstance, even when it's hard.

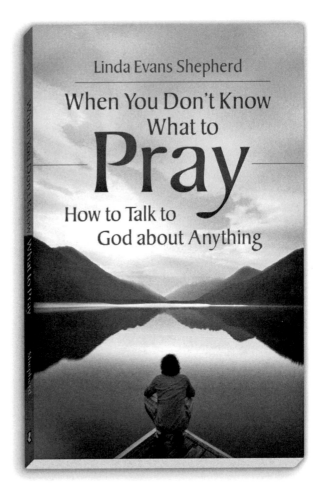